CORPSING

MY BODY &
OTHER HORROR
SHOWS

CORPSING

MY BODY & OTHER HORROR SHOWS

SOPHIE WHITE

TRAMPPRESS

First published 2021 by Tramp Press
tramppress.com

A CIP record for this title is available
from the British Library.

1 3 5 7 9 10 8 6 4 2

Tramp Press gratefully acknowledges the
financial assistance of the Arts Council.

Thank you for supporting independent publishing.

ISBN 978-1-9162914-6-1

Set in 10 pt on 16.5 pt Le Monde Livre by Marsha Swan
Printed by L&C Printing Group, Poland

For the Creeps,
You know who you are.

CONTENTS

PART 4: HEREDITARY

PART 5: FINAL GIRL

ACKNOWLEDGEMENTS

With every book I think, *Right, this time I'm going to do one of those incredibly classy and restrained acknowledgements pages*. And then I just flail all over everyone I've ever met because I'm lucky – I have met some incredible people and I've lured them into working with me and being my friends and when I get the opportunity to fawn publicly, well, I gotta do it.

Thank you to Lisa Coen and Sarah Davis-Goff, who took a book that vaguely resembled this one, saw a glimmer of something different, something better, something that I could be proud of and helped me to write it. The Tramps suggested that what I was really writing was a horror show; they named it; they made me feel like my weirdo interests and hobbies and predilections belonged in the book, were worthy of inclusion. And then while SDG nursed a real baby, Lisa wet-nursed this creepy baby. An editor of breathtaking talent. Thank you for the memes and the voicys and the permission to 'fuck it out the airlock' when a whole essay just had to go. Thank you also to Fiachra McCarthy, Marsha Swan, Laura Waddell and Peter O'Connell.

My friends and colleagues: Jen O'Dwyer, Cassie Delaney, Louise McSharry, Emer McLysaght, Liadan Hynes, Esther O'Moore-Donoghue, Sooby Lynch, Pauline Bewick, Poppy Melia, Siobhan Cleary, Joe Dowling, Brendan O'Connor, Gemma Fullam, Jane Doran, Teresa Daly, Liz Kearney, Yvonne Hogan, Madeline Keane, Leslie-Ann Horgan, Bill's pals, the Creeps and the *Mother of Pod* crew.

My family: Anne Harris, Constance Harris, Mungo Harris, Nancy Harris, Kwasi Agyei-Owusu, Vivianne White, David White, Hilary White, Viktorija White, William White and Triona McCarthy.

To the people who generously cheered me on in writing this book, possibly to their own detriment. Thank you Seb White, my favourite person in the world, and Mary O'Sullivan, the best (and bravest) mother in the world.

To my babies, Roo, Ari and Sonny, I love you more than you can possibly understand. To Kevin Linehan, I owe you everything.

It is not the physical or mental aberration in itself which horrifies us, but rather the lack of order which these aberrations seem to imply.

STEPHEN KING

PART 1
A HAUNTING

BEGINNINGS

The weekend that my dad died for the first time was the same weekend that my second son was born.

There were maybe hours between the events, but now in my memory they are entwined irrevocably. I want to weave them together to give them some kind of meaning. The full-throated wail of my raw and red newborn and the strained gasps of my dying father.

Looking back, I regard the ironic similarities of our two states, my father's and mine, in that moment. Nothing so closely touches the throes of death as the throes of birth.

I am crouched on a hospital bed and gasping for the breath I'll need to ride the roaring contractions. He is splayed on a matching bed just a few miles away. I am red-faced, with every contraction pushing and heaving, trying

3

to haul this baby to the surface. He is totally still, slowly sinking. He is falling away from us tethered only by a whispered thread that, once severed, will not be reconnected. We've signed the DNR, my mother and I, there will be no mechanical miracles. We do not want him wrenched back to the dreadful limbo of his world without memory or meaning, where no pleasure remains.

The last gasps of life are an inversion of the crashing waves of contractions. Birth is explosive and volatile; the final moment of life takes this same explosion and detonates it deep inside us.

That sharp October night, we were both engaged in the real work of life, the violent struggle of dying and giving birth.

My son is vividly red, damp with vernix, filled to bursting with his blood and his heat and his newly minted rage. His thick kicking legs and his bloodcurdling outrage. I love the way newborns rage into being.

My father is the opposite of this little wild thing. My father, just a few miles away, lying shrunken, almost desiccated on a high, narrow hospital bed, silent. He is bone-white and parched; I think I hear his body rustle with the slightest movement. Their two bodies haven't met, but they are bound, each offering their moments, first and last respectively, up into the same indifferent sky.

When he surfaces, my new son is dark-haired and dark-eyed. He is slapped up on my belly: a startling new person has arrived into the party of the delivery room. I hack through the umbilical cord – a length of meat, iridescent and coiled, looking alien and mythical at once. It takes a few goes with the surgical scissors before the boy is set loose. Now, the winter sun pours into the room, traffic whines by several stories down – a Friday morning like any other. The elation after birth is intoxicating. I will find I am unmanageably high for weeks.

I take a shower and watch rusty, blood-stained water wind down my legs. I feel evacuated. My thick body is hollow. I am alone for the first time in months. I am in pain but also so very high. A thought rears up: I could punch someone right now. I'm giddy with this high and lashing out sounds divine. I laugh alone in the shower and wonder why we pretend there's anything normal about giving birth. Just moments earlier, my body was gaping, yawning wide as the inside wrenched and contorted to push out a brand new fellow human being. The giddy thoughts drift and I follow them down down down, until I'm crouched on the floor. It's the most horrific shower floor of all time but exhaustion and confusion have momentarily stolen my balance.

Elsewhere, across the river in another hospital, my father dies. For a few moments, at least.

I don't know. No one has told me as I explore the particulars of my new baby, burying my head in the folds of his neck and marvelling at his various miniature elements – his strangely long nails and perfect ears. I am gorging on life. I eat and eat and eat that day. My body has done something brand new and yet also as old as time, this elemental marathon that has me demanding toast and Kit Kats every hour.

There's no hunger like it. I eat with a fierce focus every little morsel, sipping tea and guzzling the new baby smell. The baby greedily latches to my body, and we are one again.

My mother goes between these two hospital beds, telling neither about the other. The contrast between the riotous feasting in the wake of new life and the slow empty room where my dad lies must be disorientating. She braves this day (and all days) with a stoicism that verges on the pathological.

The difference between being alive and being dead is oddly not as clear-cut as you would imagine. Up until the 1950s, it was more black and white: is there a heartbeat? Are they breathing? No? Dead. However, as technology advanced and we gained the power to prolong elements of life, the line between the here and the after has blurred. With the invention of the respirator a new term was coined: 'brain death'. A body could be kept warm and breathing with death occurring only in the brain. But are we living when all consciousness is destroyed with no hope of it being regained? And if your brain dies first and your body is driven forward day by day by nothing more than reflex, well, it's no life. I've seen it.

In the last decades, medicine, mechanics and morality collided and death became both simpler and more complex. On one hand, we could pull the plug and pitch the patient into death, on the other hand, with advances came possibilities. What if we could keep them plugged in indefinitely? Could we push the air into their lungs and draw it out again, over and over until a distant time when death has been dispensed with altogether and they can be fixed and live once more?

My mother and I signed the DNR, the pleading document that asked physicians to set aside what *could* be done and instead regard what *should* be done. Which was nothing. Let him go. Please go. No more of the patient patient. No more passing time at his bedside, forgetting him as fast as he had forgotten everything.

As his illness progressed and devoured him, his body became a frightful thing. I was scared to watch his decline at such close range. I saw it for what it was, a swampy soup of death that was engulfing him, and that would flood us too if we ventured too close.

At his bedside, I tried not to breathe. I wanted to shirk that taste of sickness – a combination of bad coffee, boiled vegetables and waste. I washed my hands raw after every visit, and I scorched my insides clean with alcohol. Death can be catching.

And so he died that day for some time. But then he thudded once more to life. His eyes saw nothing, his voice had deserted years before. I can't remember the last words he ever spoke to me. They were probably senseless, but I'd trade a lot to hear them again. The monitor beside him resumed, chirping along with him for now. The nurse who had seen him come in and baulked that this skeletal creature that said nothing and saw nothing was only sixty-three, now declared dispassionately that he had rallied.

Later. It was 4am and I was back home, lying in my bed and feeding the new boy when my mother texted me.

'Are you awake?'

I knew it was my father. I knew immediately, but I didn't allow so much as a shard of hope.

I typed:

'Of course. Is it Kev?'

'They say after the surgery, his heart stopped beating. They didn't intervene. He rallied but they don't think he'll last the night.'

We made a plan. Taxi to the hospital. I crept about the dark house locating the newborn arsenal. My husband and I had a whispered conversation.

'He won't die.'

I was firm. I had to be. I couldn't start to hope. It's a strange reversal when, out of love, you are wishing, even *willing* someone to die.

I brought the hours-old baby out into the October night. It simply didn't occur to me not to. The boy was still a part of me, solely dependent on me for survival; he didn't know we were travelling through icy deserted streets towards a man he'd never know. All he knows is me. I am his location. He dwells on my body.

At the hospital a modicum of sense prevails and I realise I cannot bring something so fresh and precious into a hospital. I leave him with my aunt who has struck up a conversation in the backseat with the small unblinking being. I stand in the hospital entrance and contemplate the vast expanse between the lifts and me. On my phone there are complicated instructions to the ward. In a room somewhere in this building my dad is dying. Don't hope.

Don't hope. Don't hope.

Some part of me believes he will never die, and that I will spend my whole life watching this excruciating end.

I start slowly across the white polished floor. I cannot imagine that I'll ever get there. I have been maimed by the birth and can't walk properly. A hidden seam is all that's holding me together. I feel more conscious than ever before that I am a body and that won't go on forever. Under the coat thrown hastily over my pyjamas, I feel the ache of milk coming. This is the middle place. Between life and nowhere. This is where my dad, my mother and I have tapped out the hours for years. Trudging forward, holding ourselves, keeping a terrible pain in check, wanting a release. For all of us.

Don't hope.

I get to the lift and remind myself: This isn't it.

In the room, I touch him just in case it is. Touching him has been a monumental effort for many years now. I hate myself for this.

'This isn't it,' I announce to my mother. She is the only one who understands those words. Who understands the spell I'm trying to cast.

This isn't the room where you die, I tell him silently. *Do you understand that I wish it was?*

His dying body had become a site of pain. That's what happens with illness: it obscures the person, my dad, your child, our friends, until even when holding their hands and bearing witness to them day after day, you can no longer see any of the person they were. Their continued pitiable existence becomes a mockery of who they once were. For my dad, it was his expression. In health there was always a glint, he was a person perpetually on the verge of some mischief – some terrible pun or gleefully bad joke. Now his face had been overrun by an awful creaking smile that severed his face and killed my every memory of him.

Dying estranged us. I sensed I was supposed to be closer than ever to him, but quite honestly I was scared of him. I was afraid of being infected by all the dying. Afraid that the illness consuming him would in turn take me.

Death can be catching. Just not in the ways we think. I began dying alongside him but it was hard to tell at first. At first it looked like I was living – and living remarkably well at that. During those dying years, my main objective at all costs was to look like I was coping. I felt my entire purpose could be boiled down to one essential imperative: *don't make a fuss*. I felt I had no right to grieve, appear sad, or let myself off the hook in any way. Feeling sad about my dad seemed outlandish, like I was making a big deal, or letting the side down. His ordeal had gone on for so long that it was simply an immutable fact of our lives. We were so steeped in it, it was impossible to see or feel it pollute us. Like a slow leak of carbon monoxide, it infiltrated our lives while we valiantly made a show of being perfectly fine. This is the only way I can account for my certainty that he would never die.

Saying goodbye was awkward.

Please go, please go, please go. A silent incantation.

He would never walk again, or say my name, or know the name of the baby who was born the day he nearly died. And he would die. Despite what I believed and feared. He would die five months later.

A GHOST STORY

I

I never took his picture.

I ruminate constantly on this for the first three weeks that he is dead.

'Why would you want a picture of that?'

My husband is baffled. This I cannot answer.

My father's dying was an agonising, drawn-out horror show. It was excruciating to witness. By the end, I am sure that his heart was a muffled beat encased in a corpse. They could barely find a pulse on that last day. His limbs had stiffened; his eyes were fixed and coated with a film, his flesh hardened and intractable. I was alone with him on the morning of the day he died, his deathday, and I had the strong urge to knock on his chest. I imagined it would be a hollow knock on a dusty old sideboard. He was like a piece of furniture, heaved up onto the bed, covered loosely with a sheet around which we gathered to watch for the barely perceptible final breaths.

His mouth was the real terror. It gaped, exposing his erratic teeth and revealing how deformed his face had become during the course of that slow, creeping death. To me, his mouth was the centre-point of that room. It was the dark star around which my mother and I orbited. With its gravitational pull it drained every ounce of our spirit, like water down a plughole. It was a dense irresistible force, more compelling to me than even his staring eyes – behind those dusty eyes I could detect nothing, but in that dank mouth? There was something, something unwanted.

Why did I need a picture of that? What was I going to do? Sling his arm around my shoulders for a final deathbed selfie? Maybe. Perhaps I wanted to trivialise it to make it all seem more manageable. In the end, after one month of ruminating, I bought some chalk and I drew a picture of his dying head. It is the worst picture I've ever seen. I had to hide it away so that the children wouldn't find it and be scared. Odd that such a grotesque image should soothe me, but it did. I stopped obsessing that I hadn't taken his last picture. I now have a place to visit when I want to be back in that room. I open the notebook in my office. It contains just one image, quarantined from all the other drawings. I open to the page and it is like pushing the door to that room once more. The rubber floor is underfoot again, the stench races to greet me and I am back, strangely consoled, in a room I thought I hated.

2

He's not dead.

The morning after he died, the nursing home rang. I saw the name of the incoming caller, and my first thought was: *he's back*. The two words *he's* and *back* were both dreadful and thrilling at the same time. Dragging my breath inwards, I answered and was besieged by two opposing thoughts at once: *please, no*, and *please god*. The nursing home wanted to tell me to go to the funeral home as soon as possible. He continued to be dead, it seemed.

He's not dead. I dreamed that we were burying him alive. I woke up and realised that I had been burying him alive for three years – heaping mud and soil and debris and callous ambivalence upon him as he still-lived. While I recognised this to be true, the guilt did not begin there. I still had to burn him after all. Yes, cremation, cremation, cremation. Please. It's what he wanted / no one wants this.

But I could see the guilt; it was gathering pace on some interior horizon, a tsunami of guilt-building, consolidating and inevitable. *Come on*, I willed it to hit, but there was so much to do before then.

Planning a funeral is like planning a wedding, only in two days, on zero sleep with a lot more guesswork. He would've wanted. He didn't believe. He's dead, who cares? He hated churches. He loved the Beach Boys. In the end, I hid in the planning of the funeral. It was ironclad. No one could ask me anything beyond logistics. I wielded a clipboard – *an actual fucking clipboard* – to deflect the questions. I hugged it in front of my chest, with a pen stuck behind my ear.

'How are you?' they'd say.

'I'm great,' I'd say. 'We just need to nail down the pallbearers.'

The funeral I planned was a refuge from my grief. I clung to these answerable questions with all my strength. 'Yes' to flowers, 'no' to a cross on the coffin. I had a to-do list that I was petrified of reaching the end of. I loved The Plan. I could guess at what was beyond the funeral and I dreaded it. Give me more logistics, but don't leave me alone with myself. At one point, I told my husband that I was possibly in denial and that we should go for a walk alone away from the house to think over what had happened. We drove to the sea and I got out of the car. I had walked barely ten paces into the clear blue day when suddenly I felt untethered. I was alone in an ocean, watching the boat recede silently into the night. *Bring me back*, I begged, back to the house and the clipboard and

The Plan. I didn't know what to do without these things, you see.

Away from the clipboard was like stepping out of the pull of the earth's gravity. It was momentous and unknown out there. He's dead out there. In here, with my obituaries and my funeral running order and my pamphlets, he is not dead.

3

I am the worst, I am disgusting, I am an animal.

This conviction remains unchanged six weeks later. I am an abomination. I play a loop of memories from the years 2012 to 2014 and I hate myself. I had resented him. I hated him for his illness. I hadn't been a good enough daughter. I hadn't been patient enough and I had been unable to love him in his illness. Not the way he deserved. I had been too afraid to. I shut my love away from him. I was at his bedside but I observed him from high blank windows, keeping my love and myself out of reach. It was easier to insulate myself from my love than to feel it. I was so selfish.

4

How will I live with this guilt? This panic? This. Just this.

The guilt-tsunami crashed over me when I opened my eyes on the morning of Tuesday 23 May 2017. It was the day after his funeral. *Oh there you are*, I thought, and I had the first panic attack that I'd had in a decade. I came to call it 'My Guilt', to differentiate it from the guilt some of my other friends had told me they'd felt about their dead parents. I couldn't understand their guilt. One thing I was certain of: only My Guilt was real and warranted. Strangely the one thing they were certain of: only *their* guilt was real and warranted.

I wished I was sad. Sadness is so much preferable to guilt. At least with straight-up sadness, I could be in pain without this hangover of my own culpability. In German the word for guilt, *Schuld*, also means debt. This made sense to me. My dad was dead and now I would never be able to show him the love he was due. It would be a forever debt. A bruise of guilt and regret always tender to press. And press I would. Guilt needs to be returned to frequently, to be gouged and worried at or else it fades and I don't deserve that.

The day after the funeral I woke up searching for relief. *Fuck you*, I thought when instead of relief I found roaring panic.

Of course you're panicking today, I told myself. *You can't hide anymore, the death is here now: you can't shrug it off.*

Oh fuck off, I shot back. *Well done you and your Oprah analysis. That is grief 101, I know I have to* feel *it today!*

Of course, I thought feeling it might involve feeling sad, or nostalgic. I didn't count on feeling it to be so uncomfortable, so hard to bear, for it to encumber me so extremely. The guilt was of a choking, sick-making variety with shades of irredeemable remorse settling about me.

I made my way downstairs and came face-to-face with an abomination: the coffin arrangement. It was plonked beside the TV, a pyramid of lilies. Their perfection was offensive. They reminded me of my dad's corpse, of the way his face had been arranged, into a palatable, passable version of a human – here were these revolting things pretending to be flowers.

When I saw the made-up corpse of my dad I was aggrieved. It was immaculate, as though nothing had happened. No suffering at all. My uncles who'd been in to see him already tried to warn me. 'It's not him, you must prepare yourself.'

Ha, I thought. *I've seen this and beyond. I've sat with dying. Death is nothing compared with dying.* I looked at his refurbished face and thought, *Oh, they've whitewashed your suffering but I will never forget that sinkhole that took over your face and drained our lives.*

Then my mother and I left our lipstick imprints on its smooth, cold cheeks to give the moment some heart.

All day, I tried to avoid those damn flowers. I'd have been happier with a rotting corpse in the room. Uncles swarmed, talking memories and who had come and who was absent. A lot of talk was given over to who among the women still had 'it' and who had lost 'it'. I felt tired imagining all the funerals I would one day have to attend. I looked from one to the next: *You'll die and you'll die and you'll die.* I did the maths. How many more would I have to plan? At least now I've done the legwork. Now, I know about those black traffic cones outside the funeral homes and the going rate for a carb-heavy buffet.

I tried to lie down to escape the flowers, but I could not close my eyes without experiencing a terrible breathless-ness. Each time it was a momentary rest immediately replaced by suffocation. I fucking hated those flowers. I wanted to tear them apart.

Why didn't I? It would've been far more acceptable than any of the other impulses I was battling. Why not stamp on those fuckers and scream into their pale downcast heads? Better them than a mournful mourner.

Fuck all you mourners, I wanted to scream. *You don't know what I've seen.*

5

You left me with her.

I love her, but we needed you. 'I am close to my mother,' I tell my therapist. 'No,' she gently corrects, 'you are co-dependent. Enmeshed in one another. It's not the same thing.'

'Grief' can mean to bear or to carry. I walked behind my father's coffin with my mother; our elbows were locked and our fingers knit. I stared straight ahead at the back of the coffin that was cradled by my husband and my uncle, meshed in an embrace that is as old as life, arms entwined as they timed their steps to carry my father to the altar. *That's us*, I thought as we walked. We carried his illness, we carry this grief and now we carry each other. Just about.

Since his death, my mother has withdrawn from me some- what and, though it feels like rejection, I think she's right – it's probably what we both need at this point. We've been secluded together in a sad room for years. We're no good to each other at this moment. We're both drowning and liable to drag the other one under.

6

I cannot cry.

I don't believe in god, so I don't think that my father is anywhere. I look at the sky nearly every day and think about how he doesn't belong here anymore – this isn't his home. He's gone, and I don't know where to look for him. Each day, different levels of his goneness are revealed to me. I put on my shoes one day and think, with genuine surprise, that he doesn't need shoes anymore. I listen to a song and realise I don't know if he liked it or not. I eat chocolate and realise with shock that there is a finite amount of chocolate in all our lives.

The hitting starts almost without my noticing, really. I cannot cry, I'm reaching for tears and release but nothing comes, and so, a few times a day, I find a quiet room and I hit my head off the wall.

This is not normal. I am a little worried, but I genuinely don't know how else to live this grief thing. I desperately want to cry, but when I do, it's not the relief I think it will be. The sobs rear up and up and then they go no further. I cannot release them. They're as excruciating as the contractions of childbirth, but those surges had purpose and there was deliverance in that pain. They were waves that rose and peaked and crashed with a definitive, formidable force. Now I envy the certainty of those contractions. The spasms of grief are not so rewarding. So instead, with dry, burning eyes, I hide from the people who would care about this behaviour and I punch my head and knock it against the walls of my house.

Oh dear, this is really not normal, is it?

I need to find a very careful and deliberate way to fall apart. I cannot simply hurl my body against the rocks, because everyone loses patience for that kind of thing. I need to bash and slash and tear myself apart, but I need to do so terribly, *terribly* quietly because too many people need me to be normal. Everyone needs me to smile and be nice and be normal. I know that I am wearing people out with my mad, sad ways, so I begin to plan a better approach. The punching and hitting are fine – they momentarily quell an urge – but they are not enough. Also when you are a mother, your body is a continent on which your children dwell. They roam me with tiny hands, and smiles and kisses, and somehow seeing them encounter the evidence writ on skin of my own abuse makes me feel guilty. There's that guilt again. I give careful consideration to other ways that I can unravel.

I start with drinking because it comes very naturally to me.

7

He's REALLY not dead.

It's now been two months and life is hurtling through my body at a pace that is unbearable. When things settle down this will be better, I promise myself. I have moved to my own bedroom to lie and cradle something much weightier and inescapable than my new baby. I am now nursing my grief like a precious infant. I have shut the door to my family. My mother doesn't call me, she has her own grief-child. My husband valiantly minds our sons and his spectral wife for the duration.

I hate this new world that doesn't contain my father. I cannot stop wondering where he is. I have settled on a notion that he is in the sea. My most vivid memory of him before his mind ebbed is of him in the sea. We were swimming together and he was trying to make me understand a fundamental truth about life and the people we live alongside. We are in a small inlet in Northern Spain. It's about six o'clock in the evening, and we are doing a lazy, companionable breaststroke back to a grey pebble beach. 'You cannot take on other people and their motivations. Even if they pertain to you, they have *nothing* to do with you,' he says. I long long long to be counselled by him now.

How will I live without you? How will I live with what I've seen? How will I live knowing that death is coming? And worse, *illness*? Maybe even this particular one, the one that demolishes everything we are and makes us live right on through it.

I need to ask people more about this, I resolve. Which is what's brought me to the sea at Seapoint after work one evening. I meet my aunt who has brought me a towel and a chocolate to eat after the swim. She waits on the rocks as I wade in, feeling momentarily at home.

'Are you here?' I float and try to unclench my face. Since he is dead, my face has been in constant pain. My throat is always constricted, my jaw is tight, my back teeth are madly clamped, welded together. I endlessly swallow down the anxiety that rises inside, a wretched tide. My eye sockets ache from not crying, from *never* crying and the seized mask of my face feels like an iron maiden.

After the floating and the paddling, I talk to my aunt about how my mother is coping. We walk back up to her house in the rose gold summer evening. She is slightly ahead of me and I am explaining how I cannot keep it straight in my head that he's dead. I tell her about the two days I spent trying to imagine how decomposed his body was, only to remember that we had cremated him, his body was nowhere, it was no more. She turned back to me and took my wrist.

'Well, you know he's here—'

I feel the familiar weariness I get when confronted with other people's spirituality, but then she finishes: 'in my house.'

The world fell away then.

I felt it drop as though we had suddenly, abruptly fallen out of orbit and were now charging down through the dark vacuum. I was peeking behind the curtain. Seeing the edges of reality, seeing that it is all pretence, that death is not coming. Right then it seemed totally possible that though my dad had died, he was in fact living – no, 'living' isn't the right world – *dwelling* in my aunt's house. It suddenly seemed not only possible, but absolutely true.

While I immediately accepted her statement I did think: 'Whatever is in your house, it's not him.' I pictured it. It creeps among the flowers in her garden and peers through the back door. It looks almost perfectly like him, but devoid of that essential, fluttering thrill the living possess. It is enough like him, yet unlike him, to be utterly repellent. The uncanny valley of a corpse reanimated.

I try to imagine how it got to her house. When I last left him in the funeral home, my mother and I had forcefully kissed his cold head to leave our lipstick mouths on him. Our pictures were in his pocket. In his mouth was packed cotton, I guess. But what if we had slipped a piece of paper with the magic word into that cold, dry, dark mouth?

In early Judaism, a golem could be moulded from clay and brought to life by placing a piece of paper on which one of the names of god was written into its mouth. In modern Hebrew *golem* can mean helpless, which is how I pictured this thing in my aunt's house: helpless, but also undeniably wrong and frightening, an aberration. In folklore, the golem was controlled by its creator but often turned on them in the vein of Frankenstein's monster. While all this scared me, it also cracked open an unpleasant realisation: that I had cast my adored dad as a ghoulish thing, which is a monstrous thing to do.

My aunt opened the heavy front door. We were opening the door to a tomb. The hallway was empty but for a shaft of light shimmering with dust. I was walking through a dream. I edged around the light, giving it a wide berth as though it would burn me. My head swung from side to side, watching for it, him. The seawater running from my hair down my back was the only hint that this was real.

My aunt was offering: Wine? Tea? Soup?

'But where is he?' I asked.

She led me to the dining room. As I rounded the door – this moment of pushing open the door seemed to go on forever, even now as I type I feel like another me is some-where still pushing open that door – I held my breath, steeling myself for what I was about to see. Oddly I had felt no such discomfort in the funeral home rounding the door to his coffin. I was inured to his body by then; after all for the last months of his life he had seemed dead.

I had still talked to him a bit when I sat beside his bed but more and more I had sat there reading my phone or listening to music. His death crept in at a pace so slow that while I knew the fact of his dying, it in no way seemed to be remarkable. I couldn't really *see* him in the bed anymore; he seemed more like an object, an ancient heirloom in the corner of a room around which life lurches forward.

'Forward' is not the right word either. Now, when I think of those long years I imagine that time only revolves; it does not advance.

I picture him, immovable and inevitable in his bed while we, his wife and his child, circle at a frantic speed, so frantic that we cannot see his dying, because it was not a gradual slipping away as I had imagined death to be. His death was more like an idea slowly, slowly, slowly solidifying in that bed.

And of course, my memory here is not accurate in the slightest, because at least in the beginning of the end he did still move around. He didn't know where he was, or even what he was, anymore but that persistent impetus of life pushed his body on, even while his mind fragmented, blown apart into dust. I picture his thoughts like the night sky: dying stars, expanses of unknown but maybe, hopefully, still beautiful.

Of course, all this thinking is only now, after the fact. While he was there still in front of me I did not think about him at all. It was easier that way. Though that is letting myself off the hook.

All I have learned from death is the titanium grip of true denial. It is a power beyond conscious comprehension. For the years that we were witnessing his death, I watched my mother closely and confidently pronounced her to be 'in denial'. Then with his last breath, it slammed down on me, suddenly pressing me to the floor – the full leaden weight of witnessing death. And only then did I realise, *Oh no, it was me. It was me that was in denial.*

Well, you know he's here in my house. So on and on I push the door, my lungs expanded, full of air, hoarding life.

He is, of course, not here. It is his ashes she is talking about. They are sealed in an imposing box on a walnut

32

table, backlit with a celestial glow by the window over-looking the garden. My aunt has laid out an informal shrine for the box. It is resting on a beautiful print, which I later recognise to be a Tibetan *thangka*. *Thangkas* are created to make tangible the highest state of consciousness, the Buddhist spiritual path. They are sometimes called 'maps to enlightenment'. A few talismanic objects are arranged nearby: a framed photograph of my dead grandparents; the cards on which my aunt had written a version of the story of his life and read from at his funeral; and an incongruous snapshot of me aged about eight or nine covered in pigeons in Trafalgar Square. In her cards, she had transformed his illness into a fairytale coma, a magical sleep – a spell to be broken by death.

It was a beautiful story.

Not like this story.

CORPSING

In my life to date, my responses have rarely fit the situation. I find responding appropriately is challenging. If the moment calls for sincerity, I want to revolt. I want to make jokes. I make jokes that I find funny, but no one else gets. Funny comes first above all else when I'm trying to create something. I complain to my husband about how this book I'm writing about grief and addiction is 'minus craic'.

'It doesn't all have to be funny,' Seb sighs, because living with someone who is in a perpetual state of trying to be funny is, presumably, pretty horrendous. Like sharing a space with a precocious stage child.

'But if it's not funny then I'm just boring people with my crap life.'

Funny makes things worthwhile. Funny gives plain women value, we've been told. Funny is also perfect for distracting us from real life – *that* absolute buzz-kill. I have an annoying tic. I cannot be placed in a group situation without a knee-jerk impulse to try and entertain everyone. It's a grotesque pathological type of attention-seeking.

'You don't have to be funny here,' the psychiatrist offers in a bored voice after I land another pithy take on how my suicidal thoughts are abysmally banal and unimaginative.

Oh but I do, Doctor, the creepy stage-school child who drives my brain whispers back.

After I got sober, I went to a kind of group therapy thing. It's perhaps not the best move for a manic extrovert such as myself. I immediately begin to rate myself against how many laughs I can get from the room during my sharing. Even in this place of honesty, I can't help myself; I'm playing for laughs. Being funny is just so much preferable to being honest. It's easier. You can seem open and engaged, but really it's an emotional sleight of hand to ward off real connection.

While my dad is dying, I write a bit of comedy about death with a view to performing it for an open mic night. Thankfully, I can't remember many of the 'jokes' but there was definitely one about how in near-death he had finally reached his 'goal weight'. I think I wistfully described him as 'Victoria Beckham-thin'.

The truth is that watching death is not all that funny. It's frightening. It smells bad, it leaves a taste in your mouth. It slips into your life, it clings to your clothes, it infects you, and if you sit with it long enough your humanity starts to atrophy. And then you laugh inappropriately because the goalposts have changed. What's funny has changed. The feel of your life has changed and the things you need to do and say to stave off the dire truth of your situation mean you are constantly out of step with other people.

People flinch at my glib comments. A well-meaning acquaintance asks after him and I belch out a ghastly joke, having dispensed with so many of the niceties we persist with to keep the social equilibrium intact. Anything rather than cry or explain that death is infesting me.

An infestation. It reminds me that at a molecular level, we are all a shimmering mass of atoms, brushing up against strangers and loved ones, park benches and pillows at night, melding on this atomic plane for fleeting or even prolonged periods. So sometimes I am fully a part of this keyboard; each time my fingers hit a key, the key absorbs a bit of me and I of it, the same when I bury my face in my baby's hair or hold the hands of my dying father. We cannot perceive this connection. In fact, what our eyes can tell us of any given moment is limited; in many ways we are ridiculously ignorant, as ignorant as a joke about a dying man wasting in a bed.

Perhaps because of the unruly atoms, during his dying days, I believe I have caught some of his death. I believe myself to be dying in time with him. And in a way I am. I am murdering myself. And our respective illnesses have some commonalities. Loss of memory and cognitive function – his tragic affliction meted out by what? The universe? Some trick of genetics and nature? Mine is meted out by me. I lift the glass and greedily suck down every drop, but I don't control this thing. Like my dad, I am lost, roaming the empty rooms in my head, groping in the dark. It's a punishing search for numb comfort to cope with these unremarkable days.

During these years, I can't remember my real dad at all. I sit by him and try to summon one single thing about him before his illness swept in. This illness is a thief and a liar. It ransacks my happy memories until, just as my father can no longer recall me, I can no longer recall him. He has been a helpless drag forever. He was never beautiful, and strong and wise and funny.

I sit by his bed and berate myself for not doing more deathbed-appropriate activities. Like what? Like fond remembering. Hand-holding. Crying for him. Loving him. I know that tapping out the minutes until I leave again is not the proper way to do this death thing, but I also cannot cannot cannot allow myself to feel the full force of his dying. I'm too afraid to, so I keep myself gently anaesthetised to the facts of him.

The facts of him depend on when you visit. In 2014, he is mobile but erratic, still living at home. He remembers my mother's name but not mine. He is drifting into psychosis, but we don't know it yet.

One day, he wrenches my first baby's pram away from me and begins to storm across the road towards the seafront. He is more *wielding* than wheeling the pram in which my two-month-old baby is sleeping. I run after him, tugging at his arm to slow him down and get us all safely across the road. Once on the other side, my dad shrugs me off – he is still strong and fit – and gives me a penetrating, suspicious glare, his features rearranging to become a face I've never seen before. The charge of adrenaline buzzes in my arms and my new scar from the recent birth thrums uncomfortably, reminding me that running is not an option. I'm stuck here. I always figured that's why birth injures us, to prevent us from fleeing.

Worse than the burning pull of the healing wound is the gush of fear at this sudden turn in events. I recall a moment from many years before, when a man I thought was simply pestering me suddenly reached out to push me against a wall. It took about twenty seconds to register the new reality: this stranger wasn't just annoying me, he wanted to hurt me. Now, here beside the sea, the person who had loved me, who'd never shown me anger or contempt, was a person I needed to shield my child from. And my child, a downy stranger who torments me – being as he is the site of a new and fathomless anxiety – needs my protection. I'm trapped in this fearsome situation, loving them and fearing them both equally.

Later that year, my dad's psychosis has gone, but with it goes his more lucid moments. Now he lives in a psychiatric ward among people with eating disorders and depression, because hospital bureaucracy states he is too young for the dementia ward. We walk around and around the corridors that overlook a bright interior atrium. I see someone I went to school with. My father baffles the other residents, but they are kind. He greets cats that are not there. He welcomes me with a hesitant recognition and I remind him of my name and who I am. The doctors are struggling with his meds and some days he seems catatonic. I'd take a bit of that. In this ward, I bring him ice creams every day, which he devours unselfconsciously, like a baby.

I feed him from the spoon, just as I'm doing with the baby at home. The bleak art of spoon-feeding an adult. I detest feeding my father. The food is disgusting, the whole process a cruel parody of nourishing. My handsome, refined father now gobbles from my proffered spoon and inside I howl with the injustice of it all.

In 2015, he is in a different place, a nursing home. We still feed him ice cream. He still moves about with some help. He has a large chair on wheels with a seat belt, and we bring him to a special visiting room where I can unleash the baby who is now a rowdy toddler. I bring a box of toys and the child plays, unconcerned with the man we come to see. My dad mostly appears not to see the baby, or my mother and me. Occasionally, he twitches to life. One day his leg gives an involuntary jerk and lightly kicks the small boy. My cosseted son looks affronted and my mother and I laugh. We gossip and talk work and life until it's time to go home again.

I take my dad back to his room and bestow whatever affection I can bring myself to. I stroke his face and kiss him. I don't know why but this is tremendously difficult. I can hardly bear to do it. Detachment is my only defence. I cannot allow him and his slow torture to engulf me. I race home, eager to get back to my real life, and commence my routine. I open wine 'for dinner'. I pour the first large glass and drink it down in one. Then I pour two normal glasses and take them in to my husband and pretend the first never happened. I pretend to him, but most especially I pretend to me.

In 2016, same nursing home, different ward. I am pregnant again. I leave the alcohol when I'm pregnant. Oddly it's not a huge struggle for me, in those months of calm waiting I find I am sated finally. No need for drinking, I am full instead of something unbearably precious and sweet. In this new ward, I perceive a shift. I think this is when the dying truly sets in. A death of this kind has a way of setting in, eventually tipping the balance until, although the heart still beats, one is more dead than living.

This ward is the last stop, the residents are emaciated, keening in beds and chairs in the communal room – the existence of such a room – a *communal* room – is a bleak farce; every one of them is now completely entombed in their illness. Alzheimer's corrupts the brain so irrevocably that the body becomes a cell; the last days of life spent in a desperate solitary confinement. My dad is never kept in the communal room. His bed is in the corner of a large room of four. His possessions have dwindled by now. At the age of sixty-three, he no longer owns shoes. Or shirts. Or books. His paltry wardrobe is pyjamas, jumpers, t-shirts. He doesn't even need underwear. Sometimes these are the things that can shock us most about someone dying. He doesn't need shoes. He doesn't need a coat. He will never go outside again.

When the new baby comes I bring him with me. I get the sense that my dad and this baby are already acquainted, perhaps because the baby's arrival coincided so closely with my dad's tiny momentary death. I picture them in some airy celestial waiting room working out the logistics of their entrances and exits.

My older son no longer comes, as it doesn't seem fair now that he is growing up and becoming more aware that something is very wrong with my dad. The baby brings a gust of hope into the dying place. The nurses all love to come and gorge on the baby, a small respite from tending to the suffering. And the baby gorges on me as I sit with my dad. I am depleted beyond anything I've ever felt before. I am being ravaged by two opposing forces, grief and new love. Each thing is more demanding than I can manage, so I have retreated once more. I have retreated into a new realm of numbing because my version of drinking is not compatible with breastfeeding. Instead I am enjoying the pain medication prescribed by the hospital and trying not to think about how much I'm relying on it.

In 2017, he is dead. It is May and I dispense with breastfeeding in favour of drinking. It's really all I can come up with to do in this new world that doesn't contain him.

The howling hunger is back and also I have new ills to treat: guilt, rage, boredom. The current of my fucked-up life runs quietly beneath my normal life. My drinking when it's at its best, its absolute optimum, makes my days manageable. But I'm not participating in the world. Not properly at any rate. I feel like a corpse myself. Like a corpse done up to resemble the person I was. My make-up is heavy, hiding the perpetual cycle of drinking and hangovers. I am a sweet-smelling corpse; perfume masks the sickly decay seeping from my alcoholic body. I always chew gum. I've switched to white wine for practical purposes. No staining.

I have all the appearance of functioning, I am a high-functioning corpse. However, I don't really *feel* things, which, I suppose, is my goal. I search for sadness in the months after his death, but come up with nothing but guilt and relief that I no longer have to watch him die, and then further guilt at the relief. The main objective is to very carefully and quietly drown this life in wine. In the main, this works exceptionally well. I am an excellent secret drinker. Only occasionally does my careful management of the situation slip from my grasp. In other words, I corpse.

In theatre, 'corpsing' is breaking character on stage, usually by laughing. On the stage of my little drama, I corpse by revealing my true hungry nature. I go on a Sunday

44

afternoon playdate to a friend's house so our kids can play, and I bring a bottle of wine. I pour us each a glass and then focus every shred of my attention on sipping the glass s l o w l y. Even still, I'm finished long before her. I top us up and persist in attempting to be a relaxed normal drinker but it really is futile. It's like trying to stop water from draining down the plughole. Eventually my concern for appearances is eroded and I give up. I drink the rest of the bottle myself.

I made pathetic efforts to hide what I was doing from her, but given we were in the same small kitchen, our children playing in the room next door, I presume I was embarrassingly obvious. Thankfully there is a cure for embarrassment and shame. I leave and buy another bottle on the way home.

In the days after this afternoon, I metabolise the shame and make note of the fact that I must temporarily suspend this friendship. This is what I do at this time: I try to spread my dysfunction around so no one can compare notes. In 2017, the alternative – to recognise that my corpsing at a playdate and downing a bottle of wine mid-afternoon is not the behaviour of a normal drinker – is unthinkable. I know on some level that this thing is getting bigger than me and that the stench of decomposition is starting to taint my meticulously compartmentalised life. But I just cannot admit there is something more wrong than the obvious things that are wrong. And as much as I think drinking alone daily is becoming hard to manage, I also cannot countenance not drinking. Being without it is just not an option. The pain of continuing must outweigh the pain of stopping before I'll ever consider burying her: the wine-sodden corpse.

THE ASHES

The thing about death is that it can be pretty funny. As much as it is a horror story, it is also very often pure slapstick. One of the more amusing aspects of the corpse is the way we dispose of it – so much pomp and ceremony to detach ourselves from the knowledge of what we are really doing here, which is essentially burying a very large piece of meat before we have a major mess on our hands. Quick, bury it! Before anyone has to see the decay and know how frail and human we all really are.

There's a bit of a blind spot in our knowledge – the bit between the last breath and the posthumous makeover is murky territory. What do they do exactly? Without insight, these ablutions become half-imagined theories borrowing from what we know of taxidermy and horror movies. Unless you're in the business, you don't really know what goes down at that point. Is there draining? Salting? Curing? Because I'm a life-long sicko – morbid to the bone and born and bred on rotten.com – I know heaps about murder, dismemberment and disposing of a body *unlawfully*, but virtually nothing of the business of death, an entire field of industry that works 365 days a year (presumably those fridges are never turned off), carrying out essential work but rarely in any kind of visible way.

Before my dad, I'd only spent a minimum amount of time with a dead body. It's funny, but no matter how solemn the moment, you still mostly expect the thing to pop up for one final, vaudevillian fright. Especially for a prankster like my dad, there's no way he'd miss the opportunity for a camp scare. I imagined him requesting we skip the coffin altogether and simply sit him up in the front row of his own funeral, the queue of uneasy mourners offering us condolences while his cadaver smiled manically beside us – this, by the way, I can't resist telling you, is really a thing, more popular than you might realise. New Orleans socialite Mickey Easterling sat with a glass of champagne and a cigarette at her own funeral while David Morales was dynamically posed on his Honda motorbike, presumably ready to speed to the grave. My mother and I went with the more traditional cremation and had a sing-a-long funeral.

The question of the ashes hung over us for more than a year after the cremation. The ashes bookended our every interaction.

'We must do something about the ashes,' one or other of us would implore at the beginning and end of nearly every conversation we had.

Eventually we decided to take a holiday together and, to underscore the misery of that prospect, it was understood that we would incorporate the scattering of my father's ashes into the trip's itinerary.

The holiday started in predictably farcical fashion when, on the first morning of the trip, I asked where my dad was, only for my mother to return from her bedroom looking sheepish and holding a Saxa Table Salt container.

'Okaaaaaay.'

'You're never to write about this,' she warned as I laughed. It is perilous to know a writer, even worse to be stuck with one of your own making.

'I couldn't even. It would be too ridiculous to put in a story,' I reassured her. And yet, whaddya know, here we are.

The Saxa container had been selected because of some trepidation at bringing the ashes on an international flight. The bureaucracy of death is surprising. And while, for sure, it was a deliciously bonkers receptacle, straight out of a Coen Brothers' film, I'm pretty sure she didn't consider how utterly apt it was. As we stood on a terrace with vast blue overhead, blinking in the sun and at the foot of the salty sea, I understood what the ones we love do for us. They provide the essential seasoning for our lives; they turn an otherwise disparate (and sometimes desperate) collection of meaningless events into something rich and full of depth.

Salt of the earth – that crime of cliché – is an utterance often produced when speaking of the dead: 'He was the salt of the earth.' No one would accuse anyone I'm related to of this. We're all a bit too, well, salty for that cosy epitaph. But as I regard his latest incarnation: My Dad, The Table Salt – I allow that my dad was as essential to us as salt is.

When eating a well-seasoned dish, you are not supposed to taste the salt; it should be added only in enough quantity to balance the other flavours, to bring them into harmony. That is what life is like when you are loved by a wonderful person. So much of that time you are unaware of them, of the calming influence that they quietly bring to your days. When a meal is unseasoned, even someone who barely cares about flavour will know by instinct that the spoon is lacking something essential. Salt is among our seven basic taste senses. To a chemist, salt is what you get when positive and negative ions enter each other's orbit. To us lay salt-enthusiasts, it is the eminently satisfying white crystals left behind when seawater evaporates. It contains sodium, which the human body needs to survive.

In essence we need salt to live, so now I find I'm getting irritated by my mother's Saxa tub. It's pretty heavy-handed symbolism is what it is.

'If this was in a TV show or a film, it'd be too much,' I complain. 'You've gone mad on metaphors. I suppose we're going to sprinkle him in the sea "from whence he came".'

'I'd had a couple of ideas,' she mutters.

We go down to the supermarket to buy the makings of the meals we always ate in that apartment looking out on that sea. Cured meats, fresh peaches, mozzarella and herbs, tomatoes and garlic. I do the cooking, although 'cooking' is a stretch, it's more of an assembly job. I grill the bread and rub it with garlic and oil, then cover with chopped tomatoes. Salt and pepper. Then in the hot pan I sear the peaches and scatter them on a plate with torn mozzarella, fresh mint and balsamic vinegar. A little lighter with the seasoning here; adding salt to the sour of vinegar can be a bit much.

On a separate plate, I arrange the prosciutto and salami with Manchego cheese, mini cornichons, and a small ramekin of honey. These are not all flavours of the region. They are more of a family portrait – it's the picnic I have

51

enjoyed with my family in a variety of locations over the years, but it was born here in his place. The elements are not our creation by any stretch but I can call up each of us approaching this meal. I roll salami around a cornichon and dip it in the honey. My mother loves the peach salad and will always without fail comment that the mint 'makes it'. My dad was a gorger through and through and would dedicate himself to the cheese.

We sit down to eat; no one moves to occupy his chair. I make to sprinkle my lunch from the Saxa container – if we're going slapstick, we're going slapstick. Also I know for a fact my dad would've made the exact same joke.

'I'll never hear the end of this,' my mother moans.

'No, you won't.'

Scattering ashes is always going to be fraught with comedy. It just has to be somehow, otherwise it's too bleak.

Like any ash-scattering party, my mother and I set out to a remote, wild and beautiful place and attempted to be solemn while also desperately trying not to … well … ingest my dad. With hindsight, setting the ashes in concrete would be a far better approach. Why, in all this time, haven't crematoriums grasped the concept of weather?

It transpires that my mother and I have quite divergent ideas on scattering ashes, and on this holiday in general. I presumed we would be doing a single scattering. Definite.

But it soon became apparent that we would be doing a multi-day, multi-destination ash-travaganza, like a Celtic Tiger wedding, only for the disposal of a loved one.

My mother has a list of locations, apparently each more windswept than the last. We try to reminisce and say meaningful things at the various picturesque settings, but our grief is still very young and unformed. We struggle to put meaning to these rituals, spluttering out sentiments that feel impotent because we've yet to manage the sincerity required of us. We're not good at picking through the wreckage to exhume memories and anecdotes. It strikes me that this is exactly why there's a whole industry devoted to marking a death. Priests and officiators are basically gravitas for hire, elected as arbiters of all things life and death to keep us anxious and unhinged civilians from bungling it up.

This town is full of my dad's doppelgängers. Everyone has a time and place in life that is most them and this blissed-out ex-hippy haven on the edge of the shimmering ocean was his. His uniform when he repaired here year after year for two decades was shorts, deck shoes, and a broad tanned back. I'm sure he put on a shirt every now and then but in my memories he is always topless, vainly flaunting his greatest asset, the natural tan that was the envy of the family. Around every corner in this place is a man like him walking the cobbled streets bringing bread home for a lazy lunch on the terrace. My dad seemed to belong here as much as any of the native Catalonians. I can see him diving off every jetty and rock that juts into the ocean and it is here that we are leaving him.

In twenty years of holidays in this town, our culinary rituals have never changed. When we go out, it is to the same two restaurants we always did: one owned by a beautiful older Spanish man who always greeted my dad like an old friend. Here we ate the same set menu for twenty years and now, during this ashes-scattering trip, we make the same little pilgrimage to eat their locally caught sea bream and simple boiled vegetables.

The other restaurant is a pizzeria with gazpacho and the same brand of breadsticks unchanged in all the time we have been coming. The owner is a brisk business-like woman who also has a hand in local politics and always reserved a special camaraderie for my dad that she simply did not extend to others. As the years passed and my dad's illness gathered pace and began to permeate his every interaction, she perceived the subtle shifts and hesitancy in his demeanour, absorbing the knowledge that this man was still there but somehow not, not entirely. The year we arrived without him for the first time, she understood without explanation. The pleasantries she reserved for him did not pass automatically to us by dint of our being his next of kin. That was a relationship he shared with her and her affections did not transfer to us: even I, his child, was just a cheap imitation in terms of looks and lacking in any of his easy charm. Plus, I didn't inherit a whiff of that spectacular tan.

As I have sat with the grief longer, I have gradually mastered thinking of my dad again, beyond the filter of illness and uncontaminated by my guilt. In my thoughts he is always here by the sea in Northern Spain. It has taken a while to understand why but I realise it's because his illness never quite made it here. The last year we brought him here he was a muddle for sure. We couldn't leave him alone for a moment, of course. But he could still dive confidently into the blue, though whether this was a conscious act or pure muscle memory, who can know?

One night on that trip, he sat in the pizzeria, hunched in the corner sipping water from his glass and spitting it back into a small plastic bottle he was clutching secretively under the table. What distorted logic was commanding him to hoard the water? Where did he think he was? In captivity? In danger of a coming drought? I was irrationally furious at him but I reassured him and took the bottle away. I hope I was kind but I really don't remember. Probably not.

We didn't bring him again until he made the trip in the Saxa tub, so the memories of this place are intact, spared from all the dying. In this place, he was the most alive he ever was, free from obligation or petty irritants.

He was a man who never held back from indulging. I always felt he harboured some great secret to living; he always seemed to belong wherever he was. Once my dad introduced me to Mick Jagger. His approach was skilful. We were in a pub full of people who also wanted to meet Mick Jagger, but Kev sidled up to Mick Jagger, slung an arm around him casually and said conspiratorially as though they were old friends: 'Mick, there's someone here who's dying to meet you.' Of course that someone was Kev himself, but I was pretty excited as well.

In Northern Spain, the very first year we all went he was adopted by a gang of raucous ex-pat dowagers who grudgingly accepted my mother and me as the necessary baggage that must be tolerated in exchange for my dad's funny chat and handsome presence. He fit right in to the lazy days in the sunshine, as though his satchel, suit and tie that waited back in Dublin didn't exist.

In Northern Spain, in between hobnobbing with the admiring older ladies, deflecting my mother's mocking about said older ladies and working on his tan, Kev started to school me, his fourteen-year-old daughter, in the ways of music and more broadly a little good living, which to him consisted of swimming, eating and listening to records.

Something important happens to everyone the first time they hear *Blue* by Joni Mitchell. The same goes for Tim Buckley's live album *Dream Letter: Live in London 1968*. I wish I could find out where my dad was and what he was doing the first time he heard these records but in failing that I can at least remember his face on handing me the albums to play in the little terracotta apartment in Northern Spain. It's the face I remember he had as he handed me some Manchego cheese for the first time. A sly glee, as if saying, *You'll never feel the same way about cheese again!* Or, indeed, dolphins or big yellow taxis or Jingle Bells – fans of Tim and Joni will know.

In the same small apartment, on our ash-scattering sojourn, I am crouched by the CD player picking music to play while we eat; the Saxa tub is on the table and I think some more about the human palate. Or even palette – an artist's palette will, at the least, have five basic colours but nothing really happens until they are mixed. The same goes for the seven dials of taste that we experience: salt, sweet, sour, bitter, umami, fat and heat. While we think of sweet as a flavour, it is not really until it is given a contrast, such as to salt, that we can really *perceive* its sweetness fully. Like dipping Manchego in honey, which I highly recommend. In fact, I'd advise dipping most cheeses in honey, except for the gooey ones that are rich and creamy, with nutty notes that verge on sweet. Those I cut with a crisp, sour cornichon or toasted nuts.

I play some Lucinda Williams and think about lunch. I'm waiting on my mother to come up with the bread. I am also sipping warm white wine out of my water bottle, not exactly the suggested receptacle. The flavour feels stifled in the metal bottle, acid with a back taste of coffee from the last time I used it. I am still in the denial stage regarding my alcoholism. The knowledge tugs at me slightly, but I cannot conceive of facing it because facing it will require some action and what I really cannot imagine is a life without alcohol. It is up there with salt and air and water as being a fundamental requirement for existing.

Later that day, we strike out for the final resting place of the ashes. It's my mother's choice and it turns out to be an actual, bona fide graveyard.

'Huh,' is all I can manage.

'He always loved this graveyard.' She is already defensive, anticipating my questioning of this plan.

'Yes, but it's a graveyard – wherever you put him, he'll be piggybacking on some randomer's grave. You can't sublet a grave.'

We take a walk around the graveyard, which perches on a high shelf of land overlooking the sea. It isn't the kind of graveyard with headstones but rather stacked stone tombs, with commemorative plaques and occasionally kitsch memorabilia gathered on the narrow ledges. What was my mother proposing? Dusting him over another family's tomb? Leaving a little mound of his ashes on a ledge beside a tiny weathered Virgin Mary? I picture the awkwardness of that final resting place.

Crashing someone's burial plot is a fairly sizeable *faux pas* I'd say, imagining my dad without a word of Catalan trying to explain his appearance at the Figueras family tomb. He'd charm them, I guess.

My mother and I wage a whispered argument as other people step around us paying their respects and admiring the beautiful view.

'This is too bonkers,' I hiss eventually, 'and I want no part of it.' I make my way back outside the gates thinking about how grief has made my mother do some pretty crazy things, not allowing my thoughts to veer towards the water bottle in my bag with my little supply of sanity. Even more than alcoholism, in general, I know my dad wouldn't approve of this joyless consumption. Warm white wine out of a bad-tasting flask.

The next day we set the table without the Saxa tub. I dip the Manchego in honey and use a slice of salami to ferry it all to my mouth. I'm not ready to let go of the wine and I'll always worship any delicious food I ever sit down to. I eat with the sun on my face and the salt-heavy air in that warm happy place by the sea, and I feel a little freer from those death-drenched years. I breathe him in and I taste the things he loved and hear the songs he gave me. And I see him, tanned shoulders, blond hair in his eyes as he dives into the blue; *blue, I love you.*

SIGNS

I can still remember my dad's phone number. I can't remember his voice answering the phone though. I can, however, summon his singing voice. I can hear him sing the words 'the banks of my own lovely Lee' perfectly.

Along with the song I can see the half-smile that he always sang with. I can summon the other scraps of melody in his repertoire. For parties, he had a complete set-list but he dealt largely in scraps for day-to-day singing. A line here and there would trail through the house.

Have I told you lately that I love you?

I cannot recall him speaking to me, but I remember how he sang this line over and over to me for two decades. I think now it was an act of posterity on his part. An immortal lyric he set out to imprint on me, so that after he was gone, I had a shorthand for him – a summoning prayer. A sort of direct line to him.

For the last years of his life, I wrote him out of my own. I spoke about him with my mother and my husband only. I spent hours of each week witnessing the fatal entropy that was his end but otherwise I neatly edited his existence from my life. I ignored Father's Days on social media; it was easier to pretend that I simply didn't have a father than to go into the complicated truth.

I wrote about him briefly in my first book; I described the psychotic break that eventually meant he couldn't live with my mother anymore. I regretted it later when a tabloid newspaper co-opted my words and reduced the story to its starkest and most sickening details. They printed a sala-cious headline: 'Dementia Dad Attacks Family'. It was the worst day of my life. I had done that to my beautiful father. I rang the paper in frenzied tears and had them remove the article from the internet. I waited out the day, pleading for no one I loved to see the paper. I begged forgiveness from who or what I don't know. I worry there are people who saw it and still hate me for it.

I still hate me for it.

I never told my mother; I just made pleas and pacts with the universe that she would never see how I betrayed us all.

For the first year after his death, I continued to deny him. I found it unbearable when anyone tried to speak to me about him even in the most affectionate terms. It would spark a terrible unhinged anger in me.

'You look so like him,' they would say and I would flash on his shrunken final body. His shrunken final face, a bandage wound from jaw to the crown of his head to keep his jaw closed in the minutes immediately after he ended.

You don't know dick about what he looked like, I wanted to hiss. I wanted to punch well-meaning people.

'He was such a lovely, wonderful man,' they said.

He wasn't a lovely, wonderful man. How dare you? He was fucking hilarious. He was a genius. He was a brilliant mimic and a true original.

You couldn't win with me. Even I could see that.

'It's so hard,' said some. 'I know. My granny had Alzheimer's too.'

Your granny had Alzheimer's in her fucking eighties not her fifties, I silently raged.

Grief made me mean as fuck. In the first year of it when I continued to practice my committed denial of the loss, I often thought how useful an outward indicator of grief would be in society, like the hysterical Victorians and their widow's weeds and covered mirrors. It made sense. It would ward off people and their well-meaning, but ultimately infuriating, words. Death has largely been filtered out of our culture. The disproportionate outpourings of grief we now engage in when famous figures die are our main outlet for the unwieldy personal grief many of us carry – the grief that no longer has any distinct destination in this largely godless terrain.

Hilary Mantel wrote:

> A deathbed, once, was a location dense with meaning, a room packed with the invisible presences of angels, devils, ancestors. But now, as many of us don't believe in an afterlife, we envisage no final justice, no ultimate meaning, and have no support for our sense of loss when 'positivity' falters.

'In the first year, don't make any big decisions,' everyone said.

The first *month*, I started a new job.

My husband suggested that I postpone the start date, given my father's death two weeks prior. This was anathema to me. To postpone was to acknowledge that something hard and bad was happening to me. I instead planned outfits for my new life as a person with a job that was easier to define than the one I really do, which is write. I was to be a senior editor. This was something to *be* in the new foreign future. Not sad. Not smothered with guilt or choking on rage that rose like bile every waking hour. I was a senior editor on a women's digital publication. I felt proud that not only was I adding rank to my otherwise haphazard CV, I was also not giving in to the grief. I was senior editing that bullshit grief right off the page. Fuck magical thinking. I would have a year of magical senior editing.

The job was a disaster from the first day, mainly because *I* was a disaster. I was used to working by myself, used to autonomy and sole control of my time and schedule. I wasn't used to an office with the attendant politics and essential niceties. Niceties I'd have struggled with even had I not been temporarily demented by grief. I knew I would have to extract myself, but I couldn't cope with the idea of playing the recently bereaved card. Of admitting that I was being rocked by something so banal and fundamental as sadness.

The job was south of the city centre and for three months I rode my red racer out along the coast to the office. I frequently stopped to swim in the sea on the way there in the mornings or would meet my aunt for a dip on the return leg. It was lying on my back in the sea that eventually I stopped editing thoughts of my dad and instead began to expand on them – letting the memories come. In the sea, I felt safe to think of him. The water held me, and the cold numbed me to the pain that came with thoughts of him and everything that had happened. The water's edge at Seapoint was populated with men like him, tall strong bodies with veiny feet diving into the dark water.

As I edited by day – everything from my demeanour to the words on the screen in front of me – I began to spill words haphazardly at night. I was writing the first draft of what would become a novel, and there in the midst of it emerged a portrait of Kev, insistent and undeniable. The man's name was Miles and he loved swimming and life and his only daughter. I hated being so obvious, so I changed Miles's passions to theatre and restaurants, though there were many overlaps with Kev, who also loved eating and movies and music and television and even acted in plays when he was younger. The details were irrelevant anyway; Miles was a faithful rendering of this man I'd loved and lost and whom I'd failed terribly in the years of his illness. So I couldn't speak about him yet but I could write about him, which has always been my pattern.

Now with hindsight, as you can likely gather, I am very much enjoying the paradox of my daily editing and nightly purging during this bleak summer in 2017. The other nightly purging of this time came in the form of unsettling dreams with which I would never normally bore anyone, except that one of them so perfectly articulated the physical sensation of grief that I actually woke feeling quite awed at the ingenuity of my subconscious.

In the dream, I am eating a meal in a restaurant with my mother. My dad lies dead on the floor beside us. I am struggling with what I've been given to eat. My plate is piled high with animal pelts, which I have to painstakingly cut up and force-feed myself. The sensation of chewing on the fur and pushing it to the back of my throat to dryly swallow is the exact feeling of life in the time of grief. The feeling of fur infiltrating my mouth and my body is the very wrongness of death and that joyless meal is the essence of tapping out the days of loss. There is no cure, no respite from the grief. You cannot edit it, you cannot deny it, you cannot go around it; the only way out is through.

On Valentine's Day 2018, when he is nearly a year dead, my phone rings late one night. I don't see the call until the morning. It is my parents' house phone saved under the moniker they went by among family 'MerKev'. They had met as teenagers and their togetherness was an immutable fact to everyone who knew them. Some of Mary's brothers were so young when my teenage dad started calling to their house that I suspect they don't remember a time before him.

On this morning, I startle at the name because it has been such a long time since I'd seen or thought of it. It dates from before my dad was sick. During his dying years, my mother had unhitched from their collective noun and reverted to being Mary. She'd always been independent, but now she was for the first time in four decades a completely solo entity. On this day, I am also concerned because my mother never uses the house phone. Like most other house phones, it is a fossil on the hall table. After mobiles, my parents all but gave up answering it because anyone who called it, they reasoned, was probably not worth talking to.

I ring her back – on her mobile of course – and apologise for missing her. She has no idea what I'm talking about.

'You rang me last night from your house phone.'

'No, I didn't.'

'But I have a missed call.'

'Well, it wasn't me.'

I don't push it with her, mainly because a thrill of an idea has begun to form. It wasn't the *Mer* in MerKev, it was the *Kev*. It was my dad ringing to wish me a Happy Valentine's Day.

Have I told you lately that I love you?

For a few days I hug this exciting development close, not wanting to undermine it by handling it too much or presenting it to others for critical analysis. Eventually, I decide to google phone calls from the dead. There is lots of coverage of people *seeing* their dead loved ones but not so many dead loved ones placing calls from beyond.

However, I do find one very promising story that supports my hypothesis and I cling to it fervently like a religious fanatic.

Dean Koontz is hugely successful writer of thrillers whose father also succumbed to dementia. One day he received a strange phone call to his unlisted phone number about twenty years after his mother had died. The line was bad but he could hear a weak voice through the crackle. The voice sounded like it was coming from very far away and said only 'please be careful' several times before the line went dead. Koontz was stunned. It was the voice of his mother. Two days later, he went to see his father in the home where he lived. When he arrived his father was very disturbed and staff on the ward were struggling to keep him calm. When he saw his son, he made a lunge for him, somehow getting a hold of a knife in the commotion. Koontz, perhaps on high alert from the call warning him to be careful, sprang into action and managed to safely defend himself and disarm his addled dad. Later, Koontz said that he was certain his mother's warning saved his life.

Eventually, I decided that I didn't need proof regarding the call. Cynicism hadn't exactly served me well, and so I decided categorically that the missed call was a sign from my dad. End of.

From that point on, I started to give in to the grief and the relief was unexpected. I took up meditating. It seemed fitting that, given I now received telephone calls from the dead, I should make space in my life for some other vaguely esoteric things.

Meditation became a powerful release. Now, I am aware that I have already recounted a dream in this essay and am dangerously nearing some kind of sincerity limit but humour me, my dad's dead. That's right, I'm playing *that* card.

I didn't know where to start with meditating, so I joined a group that gathered on Saturday mornings in a basement room beside a church. I followed the instructions being read to us. Close your eyes; allow your body to relax; empty your mind; if thoughts occur just acknowledge them and let them drift away.

The moment I allowed my body to unclench and ease, tears gathered from nowhere and began to fall, covering my face and drenching my lap. They were tears I had no awareness about. The kind of crying I'd done in the year since his death had been arid and unsatisfying. Rough, strangled cries that came with no redemption and certainly no tears. I stayed in the moment as instructed and let the tears continue, doing nothing to staunch the flow. They were mysterious tears accompanied by no inner narrative or detectable emotion. It reminded me of once seeing myself bleed while under anaesthetic. Without the pain to cloud the moment, I was free to marvel at how beautiful my rich, rushing blood was. Similarly, the sheer volume of tears were a marvel too. Had I been unwittingly storing them up? Or was I really capable of such speedy manufacture of saltwater?

For the first three months of meditating, the tears poured during every single session. All it took was the tiniest loosening of my body and they were unstoppered.

After the tears, I found I was at last ready to talk. I began to bring Kev up more. Initially I was doing a very studied impression of casual: 'My dad loved Bovril,' I would say, should Bovril make an incongruous conversational cameo. 'It was totally bizarre. I mean, what even *is* Bovril?'

Then I was throwaway, in the good way. 'The greatest tragedy is that Kev didn't live to see *Succession*. All the epic television he missed.'

It's when I miss him most, I realise. When there is an incredible new show on TV and I think how he would have talked about it with such high regard and enthusiasm. His analysis of television is a terrible loss to me. He was a child of the fifties and sixties – he had lived through the entire evolution of the medium. He used to tell me how sophisticated TV got so quickly, how its language was so universal and accessible, more so than books or theatre, that it could evolve much quicker. He loved spying the Easter eggs in films and TV; his analysis of Kubrick's *The Shining* was more rigorous than *Room 237*.

He was so widely informed that he saw absolutely no distinction between the high and low. He watched obscure indie shows and *Friends* with the same delight. He was egalitarian in his tastes and believed that cracking the mainstream was a criminally underrated achievement and anyone who thought otherwise was an irredeemable snob. He strove for mass appeal in the TV he helped make and he had some great successes, though none greater than the fact that a little boy from Cork who vividly still remembered being the first house on their road to get a television grew up to actually work in TV.

After I joined the meditation group, I met a man who had been a childhood friend of Kev's. He knew my dad as the lanky boy with a half smile and longish blond hair swept to the left. They had played together and made music. Eventually they would reunite as adults and make a TV series together that was very special to both of them. He recognised me to be his friend's child and he said the things I was now ready to hear.

'You look so like him.'

I do.

'He was a wonderful person.'

He was.

We only see each other very intermittently because the meditation group is a drop-in situation, but whenever I see him, I beam.

I don't tell him this because it seems an unfair burden but when I see this man, I know he brings with him a message from my dad. I listen to his words – if he says any – very carefully to siphon off some private meaning of my own. And on the days I see him, I feel buoyed.

The meditation time becomes a time in which I visit with my dad. I drop out of my daily life and visit a place few people know about. When I'm back, I tell no one where I've been – in this way, it is not unlike the hours I spent by his bed in the hospice. In other crucial ways, it is vastly different. We meet now by the sea: the air is fresh and salty, unlike the soupy air of the hospice. He is restored. Tanned and sun-bleached, which to me always seemed to be his natural state. Another beach boy diving into the surf. And we swim and we chat and I remember him as he was.

A little while ago, my friend told me how she asked her dead people to send her signs. 'You have to be specific,' she counselled. 'So you know it's really them.'

What can be more specific than him giving me a ring on Valentine's Day and leaving his childhood best friend lying about for me to stumble across? Though admittedly, I didn't request those signs. Instead I've cobbled together a language of his love, a kind of abstract melody that wends through the days I live without him. Magpies gathering, rangy weathered foxes that steal across my night-time path, an expression of his stirring on my second baby's face, the quiet voice of his friend and the refrain ...

Have I told you lately that I love you?

PART 2
SWALLOW

I GET IDEAS

I am writing these stories slowly and in a scattershot fashion. It's not the way I usually write, and it is terribly frustrating to me. The clicks and turns and levers in my head have slowed unbearably of late. I can't remember things. I pick up thoughts and put them down again, only for them to vanish completely. I feel around in the darkness to retrieve the thing and it's gone, replaced only by a queasy dread that all is not well in my head.

It's been five weeks since my latest breakdown and the medication seems to have settled things in the way it is meant to. I haven't hurt myself or thought of suicide in several weeks. So that's a win. On the other hand, my head feels like it's barely grinding forward. While on some level this is a relief to me – most of the time, my mind goes too fast – I'm now in a constant state of badgering myself to get on with things.

I deliberate endlessly about what is Normal Me and what is Medicated Me and wonder if I could just get back the bits of Normal Me that work (my memory, my drive, my orgasms, regular showering) and ditch the other stuff. The 'other stuff' is a variety of things that for a long time I'd convinced myself were not even happening: uncontrollable rages, self-abuse, extreme mood swings, hyperactivity and profound feelings of blankness.

I realise that this breakdown has been more gradual than previous ones, coming on without my even noticing. Like every woman, I'll put up with untold amounts of crap. I had tolerated and ignored the noxious rage simmering just under my skin, until it swelled to such unmanageable proportions that I needed to lock the door behind me and hit myself in the head. I had compartmentalised that behaviour so expertly (that's a weird humblebrag, right?) that I barely knew that it was happening.

The creeping knowledge that this was not normal sighed by the door as I dragged my nails across my scalp and hit my head against the wall, harder and harder until for some reason it gave me peace. Then I'd run the bath, check my reflection for marks, and start the arduous process of getting my children into the warm soapy water.

I open my mouth to call my babies and the voice that emerges sounds normal but separate from me somehow.

The hot running water creates a perfumed mist and as the boys enter the scene changes; a ripple of reality spreads through the room. For a moment, I can see all that this small tiled room contains. My older boy is lean and wiry; he pushes past me and vaults into the water of his own accord. The younger boy perches on his fat baby feet at the bathside, demanding I lift him in. I hike him up and into the bath where they wrestle and fight and ignore each other in a chaotic fashion that never stops being awesome, in the true sense of the word.

I sit on the toilet lid and again for a moment I grasp all that this room holds: while the babies splash and fight, in the corner another me – from just moments earlier – crouches on the floorboards, raking my nails across my body and clawing at my loathsome self. The proximity of these two things is dreadful. I'm scared the twisted animal in the corner might find the lively, happy flesh of my babies. I am an animal; I am repulsive.

Their shouts wake me from the bleak dream. Time for shampoo and cleaning of little pink ears and robust, proud baby bellies. I watch my hands as I rub their backs. I regard them with suspicion. It's reasonable: these hands have turned on me, done terrible things – they have done boring things too and some good, I hope, but it's hard to trust them. Hard to trust myself.

I pick up the idea that all this is not normal and drop it like it burns. And then it's gone again for a time. It occurs to me how odd it is that I can do these things to myself and then, in the very next moment, I can wash a baby or reply to an email. Does that make my mad ways more or less odd, I wonder, and then briefly enjoy the absurdity of that line of inquiry.

I seem incapable of grasping that all is far from well in my head, never mind attempting to help myself. I probably could've gone on like that indefinitely, but then I began to get ideas. And this, I sense, is where I could really lose you now. These ideas are not your friendly neighbourhood 'let's meet for brunch' kind of ideas, but more a 'nothing's real, what if everyone I know has never been born and I am actually in a coma and my life is not real but actually just one long coma dream?' kinda vibe. Ugh god, I hate telling people my ideas. I sometimes picture my psychiatrist like an editor offering feedback:

'Sophie, this delusion just feels really derivative. Maybe in need of a little more development?'

The idea that spurred me to seek professional help in this particular instance was timely if nothing else. It was Halloween, and a low-grade concern had started up somewhere on the outskirts of my mind. A concern that I was possibly possessed.

Uh huh.

I know, I know. It's not great.

The idea remains peripheral for a few days, the volume on it is turned down but it hums along quietly while I file copy for work and make dinner and see friends. But gradually it starts to increase, persisting and amplifying at all times of the day and night. Is this what's wrong with me? Has a nefarious entity stolen into my self and taken control of the monstrous hands?

Important sidenote: Perhaps you're a believer in demonic possessions and you're sagely nodding along right now. That's fine, but I do not believe in these things, so to suddenly be incredibly preoccupied with this, is, well … it's not great, is what it is. It's terrifying.

Soon the possession theory is like a weather system in my head, obscuring all the other thoughts. Seb is away at this time, and one night the obsessive thinking tips over into a new realm. I am giving my kids dinner (shout-out to me! I made spag bol while also battling heavy concerns that I was possessed by a demon). I sit down as they eat, and I begin to feel profoundly detached from the scene. Their boisterous shrieks and inexpert use of cutlery drifts out of reach. I become preoccupied by one of their sticker books on the table, a book of emojis that all of a sudden looks deranged and sinister.

It's back, I thought. I know these feelings. While I know these feelings, every time they pour into my body I am certain this will be the time I don't make it back. People don't make it back, I silently scream. I know I'm supposed to put something reassuring on record here, but people sometimes do not return from this.

I am undone.

I gather the children. Somehow I put the dishes in the sink. I consider calling someone because I am now crazed by the thought that I will hurt my babies.

People do that, people hurt their babies, you will hurt your babies, my mind torments me.

I feel paralysed by this. I want to protect them, but I also can't bear to call my mother and tell her I am brain-sick. Again.

I put the children to bed and go to my room. My solution in this altered state is to lock the door behind me. It makes no sense, but I decide it will slow me down if in my sleep, I try to get out. It'll slow me down long enough to come to my senses.

Even in this strange lonely moment, locked away, I am aware enough to know that my senses have deserted me right then.

I go to the bed and I drown in the horror of my own head.

Then, through the debris of thoughts, comes a shock of clarity.

There's a knife in this room – two, in fact. I'm loath to admit this, but usually in my right mind I keep knives under my bed when my husband goes away. I'm not even going to bother defending this; it helps me feel safe.

'You're just handing a potential intruder a weapon, you realise this?' Seb cocks an amused brow at me.

'That's why I have the second one,' I patiently explain.

Now, in this claustrophobic hour with the danger locked in with us, I need the knives to be gone. I just about resist the urge to simply throw them out the window, afraid of witnesses to this odd behaviour. Instead I bring them down to the kitchen and survey the array of kitchen knives. There's a lot of knives there. When I'm right and normal, I cook all the time. I briefly toy with the idea of gathering all the knives and putting them out in the garden, effectively putting two locked doors and three flights of stairs between them and the *me* I'm so afraid of. The solution I eventually land on is to leave them there, go back to my room, lock the door and push a table in front of it.

Up in my locked room once more, the aftermath of the heightened state seems to drug me and I fall into a deep sleep. When I wake the next morning, there is nothing left of me inside. I feel nothing, I am weighted to the bed. I am gutted, an abandoned house. I reach for fear or even sadness and touch nothing but nothing.

Feeling ransacked and blank, I nearly miss the obsessions of the week before.

I traipse to my mother's house with the kids in tow.

'Do you want a coffee?' she asks, making toast for them.

'Yep,' I answer and then, without explanation, I go and hide in another room where no one can find me. It's a

Sunday so I don't quite know what to do. I can't call the GP to get a referral. Do I go to A&E and say I'm homicidal? Suicidal? Petrified? Possessed?

Eventually my mother finds me. In her worried face I somehow detect judgment.

'You think I'm being a drama queen, that I'm over-reacting,' I accuse. I think I'm really saying this to myself. *I* think I'm being a drama queen. *I* think I'm overre-acting, which is actually hilarious because at this point, if anything, I'm probably under-reacting.

Eventually I call the psychiatric hospital where I was treated eleven years (practically to the day) before, and leave a garbled message. My mother retreats and watches the children while I write an account of the last six weeks. This is to prevent me from lying the next day, when I sit in front of the doctor and explain why I am there. I have a tendency to lie about the extent of what goes on in my head. It's a double-sided head-fuck: on the one hand, I tell myself I don't deserve help, on the other I tell myself I'm being hysterical and other people have way worse shit to deal with. I gaslight myself, basically. Maybe that's what all mental illnesses are to a degree?

The next day I read what I've written for the doctor. It's only the second time I have ever revealed the self-harm, and the words come up like vomit. I skirt around certain things that just feel too bizarre. Concerns of demonic possession seem a bit outré for this moment in a perfectly nice doctor's office; I don't want to worry the guy. He does the things I need him to do. He sends the referral to the psychiatrist and hands me a prescription to be going on with.

The side effects of medication – the dry mouth and muted mind – comfort me. It's a familiar feeling, and besides I'm used to putting things in my mouth to fix me.

SWALLOW

The first time I pulled the plug on reality, I was eighteen and had been handed a star-shaped pill by a girl I vaguely knew in a club that I had never been to before. I was nervous but also curious. Up until that point, I'd used slightly flaccid numbing agents – alcohol and hash – to blunt life and render it tolerable. Now here, I knew, was a much more decisive and effective route. Down the hatch for an escape hatch.

That first pill wasn't incredible by any means. It was probably a dud and I was too drunk and stoned to really notice but it did give me some comfort. Much like my first alcoholic drink at thirteen, I remember the relief of discovering, *Ah, this exists. And as long as I have these things, I'll be okay.*

Drugs for me were cosy things, a place of refuge where I could take a break from being myself. I never thought to question this attitude; I always assumed that every single one of us was at all times dying for escape. I thought life was tapping out the leaden hours between bouts of sweet, safe oblivion. Did we not all resent being sober? Was it not a daily struggle for *everyone* to refrain from rushing at the precipice and hurling oneself joyfully off the edge? I was embarrassingly slow to realise that no, perhaps this wasn't the case for everyone.

At twenty-two, I had a bad trip that mangled my head in ways that would take years to recover from. I still live in the aftershocks of that night and have, more than a decade later, come to accept that the fits and starts in my brain will always be there.

I was in a packed tent at a festival and waiting for the euphoric up to kick in when I felt an unmistakable quake in the ground under me, like the earth was skipping and stalling. As I tried to right myself, a sudden wave of warmth rolled up my body. No one around me in the densely packed space seemed to notice. The ceiling of the tent above appeared to contract, like a lung filling, seizing the air above us. I fought to breathe, but the tent was a vacuum. I pushed through strangers to get outside, a cloying dread pouring into my body. Outside was a foreign place. Familiar objects, trees, people, even the sky above had taken on the ominous proportions of a nightmare.

I was going to die like this. The thought, once realised, took a hold of me. *I am going to die like this*.

I pushed on through the monstrous world and eventually found my tent. My panic was a roar and all I could do was curl into a ball and hope to ride out the terror. I'd experienced shades of strange on drugs before and a small sliver of reason was insisting that I was fine, I just needed the horrifying hours to pass, for my body to metabolise the drug, and then I would resurface to sanity.

Of course, hours of horror leak through at the pace of glaciers forming and the vice of anguish I was now trapped in seemed terminal. I was wracked with a sort of grief. I am going to die like this. And I did it to myself. Shame seeped up around me like floodwaters. How is shame always right there on hand? Of all the sensations nothing is ever within closer reach than shame.

Lying foetal and coiled in the tent, I stumbled into another moment. My mother and father were sobbing and I was confessing.

'I've murdered your daughter, I'm sorry. She's dead, I killed her.' They looked back at me with hate and reproach in their eyes. The hallucination lasted for minutes or maybe hours. When I came back to in the tent I was crying.

I am going to die like this.

I had grown up in the nineties when, for a time, ecstasy deaths were the bread and butter of mainstream media. Proportionally, deaths from ecstasy are relatively low compared with other drugs, but something about the promising young bodies dancing themselves into heart failure and heatstroke captured our collective imagination and fed our morbid appetites. 'Addicts' dying from heroin use weren't relatable enough – they were, more often than not, victims of a systemic culture of apathy and class prejudice. Feasting on their tragedy required too much self-reflection on the part of our society. But bright young middle-class kids paying the ultimate price for dabbling? *That* got our attention.

I groped in the tent for any sense of control. I needed to fight. I began to drink water and I rode the sensations, searching for any hint it might let up.

I am going to die like this.

And I did die like that. A death of sorts.

So what did my death feel like? Lonely. I lay with my eyes and fists squeezed tight. And I moaned quietly. I wanted to live. My head was shoved into the corner of the tent, my mouth and nostrils plugged with the fug of damp earth. I heaved oxygen, but my lungs only seemed to swell limply. My heart shook, suspended in its dark cage. It couldn't go on, surely?

Escape had always been my aim, but this final night of my old life, it didn't feel like freedom. It was a casting out. It seemed biblical. If I'd known then that my life as I knew it wouldn't exist anymore, if I'd known the intermittent torment that'd dog the next few years, I don't know if I would've fought so hard to live at all.

Luckily, in the tent that night I thought only of making it to the following morning. I didn't think of the thousands of mornings beyond that. I thought if I could survive the night, I would be fine. The drug would be out of my system and I would go back to normal. At twenty-two, I'd yet to comprehend the reality of something being ruined irrevocably, irretrievably. It's a hard thing to grasp at that age, especially for someone as privileged and cared-for as me. Nothing in my life to date had been destroyed beyond any hope of repair. I didn't understand that single mistakes can and do define your life.

Sometime near dawn, I fell into a shallow sleep, drifting just beneath the surface of consciousness. My boyfriend came back, and when the sun woke me an hour or so later, I burrowed into his familiar bulk, hungry for comfort and home. The textures of the world seemed righted. I emerged into the sharp morning light and picked my way carefully through encounters with friends. They were groggy with hangovers and it was easy to skim over my abrupt absence the night before. I moved carefully, testing the temperature of this aftermath. *Am I okay? I think I'm okay?* I began to settle. It was all over. I was fine. Shaky, but essentially fine.

The relief that ballooned in me was jubilant. The high of dodging disaster. I had peeked over the edge, into a frightening morass, and had come back from it. As I packed my things for home, I made plans to be a better person. No more drugs. No more fucking with my head. No more pointless risks. No more *more more more*.

I could see I had a problem with 'enough' as a concept. I was always seeking a second pill when the first had barely dropped. Reaching for wine, food, the joint being passed. More more more. There were no bounds to my appetite. Now I'd glimpsed what lay beyond the *more*, and I wanted no part of it.

I had packed up the tent and shouldered my backpack when the ground skipped shakily once again. My every nerve and synapsis snapped to attention. What was that? My head jerked like an animal suddenly aware of a hunter. No one around me had noticed a thing, but I could feel it all, a hurricane of familiar terror gathering speed and force before it hit. The ground beneath seemed to stutter and start just as it had the night before. An inexplicable heat was travelling once more through my limbs, and the view of my friends and tents and fields and sky around me had changed. It was a tiny, distorted landscape, powerfully sinister, just as it had been the night before.

What is happening? How is this possible? I am coming up on the drug again, but I haven't taken anything. This is not fucking real. This is not possible. How is it happening again? Disbelieving and shocked, I searched the faces around me for clues that they could feel the disturbance or see the alien distortions too, but no one looked troubled in the least. This, it seemed, was a private agony. And all the more terrifying for it. *I am going mad,* I realised. *This is what it must feel like.*

I had long-buried knowledge that some people could go mad from drugs. That some forms of mental illness had been linked to smoking cannabis. As the child of a music-obsessed father, I knew Brian Wilson had retreated from reality after LSD binges unravelled his mind. My own friend had been spiked with acid and spent years recovering. I had read the tragic story of Sid Barrett.

Now as I reeled in this awful new dawn of glass, seeing a reality I'd never thought was so fragile strain and crack, I fought to appear fine. It took all my resolve to follow my friends, smiling tensely as I tested this new world. I walked on auto-pilot to the car trying to reason my way out of the terror.

It's a bad hangover, I tried.

No it's fucking not, look how fucked up everything looks. Everyone looks like little dolls in a dollhouse.

It was true. Every single thing around me had taken on Sylvanian Family proportions. The girl beside me looked tiny and distant. I carefully reached out to try and touch her subtly. I expected the reach to go on forever before making contact but no, she was apparently right beside me.

What nightmare had I willingly swallowed?

As we drove back to Dublin, the minutes dragged by. The sensations continued. Nothing looked right and the panic in my body was unrelenting. What was wrong with me? What was happening?

Now, after years of debating my issues, I realise that if our eyes see things upside-down before our brain intervenes to pick it up and turn it right way around, then it stands to reason our brain is capable of other visual tricks and glitches.

Something about my episode had disrupted my brain's functioning in a way that was unpleasant, but also perhaps not as sinister as it felt. But to me back then, the odd visual disturbances were the first indicator that I was now mad. And once the idea of madness took hold, it was impossible to shake.

From the night of the pill, 'I've gone mad' became virtually the only thought I was capable of forming.

I am now mad. I am mad. I am madness. I am now madness. On it looped.

For months after this night, my brain stuck in this groove and nothing would release me. The very fact that I could not think of anything else but madness seemed confirmation of the madness. After all, surely it is mad to think of nothing but madness for all the waking hours of the day?

As more days crawled past, I got no better. This was new to me also. That things would not improve incrementally with the passage of time seemed unbelievable, grossly unfair. Before this, nothing had ever not gotten better eventually.

I kept a tally in a copybook. It was like those signs outside towns that proclaim the number of days since the last road accident. Thirteen days since the pill. Fourteen days since the pill. Fifteen days since I felt normal. Seventy-two days since I died in a tent and woke up into a subtle kind of hell. One that lacked the fiery theatrics you'd expect but nonetheless had efficiently decimated me, leaving little of the person I used to be.

Frightening thoughts latched to my brain like parasites. There was a litany of them on constant repeat, a *Now That's What I Call Obsessive Intrusive Thoughts* best of.

One) I was dead since the night of the pill. In 1880, the neurologist Jules Cotard encountered something he called Cotard syndrome or, even more ominously, walking corpse syndrome. He described the condition as *The Delirium of Negation*, a psychiatric syndrome wherein a mild case is characterised by despair and self-loathing, and a severe case is identified by intense delusions of self-absence and chronic psychiatric depression. The case of Mademoiselle X describes a woman who denied the existence of parts of her body and of her need to eat. She said that she was condemned to eternal damnation and therefore could not die a natural death. She eventually died of starvation.

Two) Nothing was real. Reality was a construct, all the people in my life were actors and all my memories of my life to date were false. They had never happened. The Beatles hadn't happened. World Wars I and II had never happened. The Big Bang and the Spice Girls had never happened and basically I was living in a strange projection, an artificial afterlife.

Three) I would harm my family. I was paranoid that I would stab my boyfriend while he slept, or hurt my mother, that the kind of people who did these things felt exactly like I had felt right before they lost their grip on reality altogether. These visions came like physical shocks. They felt like the thoughts of an intruder.

Four) I had gone mad. See points one, two and three.

Fear as a state of being is physically demanding. It grinds you down. Your reason, your resilience and your identity are worn away by the terror. I punished myself for being so ruined by mental illness. I waged a cold and cruel internal war.

Get a real problem, I would hiss at myself. *Think of people with real illnesses. With cancer, with horrific traumas. You don't know shit about fear!* the voice would spit all day as I continued to retreat from normal life, each small aspect of living, from washing to eating, becoming increasingly difficult in the face of all this fear fear fear.

A part of me that still struggles to find any compassion for myself thinks the voice has a point. I was once followed and mugged by a stranger in a strange city. It was frightening but thankfully a momentary and transient fear. I could escape the situation and alter my surroundings and reality. For the survivors of acute harm, it's not that simple, the trauma reverberates. Mental illness is a trauma of its own kind. It's the prism through which we *experience* reality being defective. It is the moment in the urban legend when the frightened babysitter – who has been receiving menacing calls all night – is told by police that the calls have been coming from inside the house. It is a type of mental paralysis, a cancer on your reason.

The thing I was afraid of was never being normal again. Of never experiencing a day without the auditory hallucinations, mangled vision, the disturbing flashes of violence that came unbidden and the constant, draining terror.

When the tally read ninety days since the pill, ninety days of hopelessness, ninety days of total isolation, ninety days of terror, I began to plan my suicide. Planning to die gave me a bleak sense of hope. There was one way to not have to feel like this anymore. There was a way to end this. It was the unthinkable thing. But it also offered a glimmer of respite, of peace.

The night it came to me, I had been washing up after dinner. I lived with my boyfriend, but our life had become small in the way that it does when illness resides with you. He still loved me, but I had drifted far out of reach. I was doing the dishes when I noticed that my right arm was strange. It seemed suddenly to somehow not be a part of me. I have always struggled to describe this to people. Their faces contort as I try to explain: it was still attached, I could see that. It was more this overpowering sense that the arm was not my own but instead an interloper.

In thirteen years of trying to explain this to people, I have yet to encounter someone who goes, 'Aha! Yes! The freaky stranger arm, I had that!' It's lonely when we can find no recognition in others for what we are going through. Of course it doesn't sound a million miles from Mademoiselle X and her delirium of negation. Wonderful.

I lay in Seb's arms that night and felt nothing but a strange inevitability about the fact that I was going to do the unthinkable thing. *I'm going to die next week.* As matter of fact as, *I will eat breakfast tomorrow.*

It seemed like this was the most obvious conclusion to the pathetic little life I'd had. I deserved this. I'd done this to myself. I felt guilty about what this would do to my parents and Seb. I felt sorry for them but also determined. They wouldn't know about the interminable seconds and minutes and hours of mental illness. They didn't understand what it was like to endure the mind's demolition, how nothing survives it, how days spent among the ruins are excruciating. They couldn't understand.

As some concession to not destroying them with grief, I made a pact with myself. I would try the psychiatrist before making my escape. My mother, having seen the change sweep through me over the previous months, had been petitioning me to see a psychiatrist. I had resisted thinking at the beginning that I could ride this episode out, that time and herbal tea and denial would see me through. Then, when unbearable days turned to unbearable weeks and unbearable months, and thoughts of tragic falls and sleeping pills stole along the peripheries of my mind, I finally knew I had to at least try.

I went to a psychiatrist and spilled half-truths about what I was experiencing, afraid that full disclosure would result in a locked ward or some other remedy about which I knew nothing beyond narrow-minded notions. She wrote me a prescription for antidepressants and antipsychotics.

Relief in pills was not what I wanted to hear. In my warped logic, a pill had lifted the lid on all this madness. How would more pills undo this? It seemed too risky. The irony that I was hoarding sleeping pills as a part of my final remedy was utterly lost on me at this point. All I knew about psychiatric treatment was gleaned from dubious sources, books like *Girl Interrupted*, the work of Sylvia Plath, Virginia Woolf and all the tormented women. This was at least a decade before people would begin to speak more freely about their head meds, before posts on social media revealed the myriad mental issues we are all likely to face at one point or other.

I regarded the new pills with suspicion. Growing up, I'd hear people toss throwaway comments about friends horribly altered by medication of this type. Celebrities took it upon themselves to denounce psychiatric medication. Films portrayed some psychiatric treatment as a hammer-and-nail botch-job, more likely to lobotomise you than help you. It was confusing and terrifying. For several days, two outcomes hung before me. Two different sets of pills. Go ask Alice. One pill makes you larger and one pill makes you small.

Seb seemed ambivalent about the medication, but he worried they would make me worse.

Given I'd never been worse, I decided to take the meds. At best, they could maybe turn the volume down on the roaring thoughts and hallucinatory life I'd been sentenced to. At worst, they did nothing and I could, I reasoned, then just carry on with killing myself a few days later than planned. Another few pills down the hatch. What's the difference when you're already lost? When the normal order of your mind is so corrupted you can't trust that your childhood memories are real or that your right arm is your own?

The antipsychotics were hard to tolerate at first. I found them hardly any better than my un-medicated state of paranoia and anguish. I was to take the pill at 8pm – the 'why' of this immediately became clear. Once the pill had taken effect I sagged, unable for even the most basic transactions. I learned to get the business of the day's end – feeding, washing myself – finished before the conscious oblivion. After this pill, I found even just using cutlery was out of the question. A conversation complete with eye contact? Forget it.

Oblivion was the thing I thought I'd been in search of but this particular brand wasn't the narcotic calm I'd always loved when high or drunk. This was sedation without contentment. The drug smothered the looping logic of my brain and it took away some of the sensory disturbances, but I also detected that it limited me. I no longer had access to a full range of emotions. I wasn't frightened anymore, but I also wasn't much of anything else either. A blankness came down like shutters, dividing me further from the world outside me.

As unpleasant as it was at first, I'd say this medication probably singlehandedly derailed my plans to murder myself. It didn't make me content enough to not want to die, but it definitely robbed me of the impetus to go through with it. It quieted my head. I struggled to continue with my obsessive thoughts because forming thoughts of any kind while on the drug was onerous. How could I be overtaken by the question of whether or not I was real when I could barely decipher what to do when confronted with the handle of a door?

In the end, I am so grateful for all the care I received. Though it was hard to adjust to it, medication kept me earthside, and though it was hard to tolerate at first, eventually it settled in my system and did offer respite. It was during this reprieve that the true extent of my loss hit me. For the first time in months, I had the perspective required to see that while I may not have killed myself, the me I'd known previously was, undoubtedly, dead anyway. Before the breakdown, I was boisterous and loud and self-assured. I was probably annoying to a lot of people. I revelled in my health, not even aware of how robust I was as I veered through days and nights devouring people, food, booze and drugs. I was selfish and I hurt people. I did endless stupid things in my quest for living. I broke into building sites and ran on tiptoes on the edges of high rooftops. I jumped in the ocean so full of booze and ignorance, I deserved to drown. I was so sure of myself that consequences, death or injury quite simply didn't apply to me. I was young, basically.

In the wake of the breakdown, with the mania of the previous months finally tamed – for the moment, at least – by medication, I could begin to survey the wreckage of myself. It is quicker to say what had not been profoundly altered in the months of brain sickness. My hair was still blond, my eyes were blue and I stood 5′ 8″ in bare size 8 feet. I still had the birthmark in the shape of coral sprawled across my upper back. It is like a birthmark in reverse in that the shape is demarcated by flesh without pigment, rather than in red or brown. The mark surfaces vividly in cold sea or after a hot shower. It is an absence. Just as I had become.

What else of me remained? Little. My gait was changed; I moved with a new hesitation. I struggled to inhabit my life, conversation flowed and rushed around me and I could not grasp its meaning. My slowness to answer meant that fewer questions came my way. I lost my independence: I moved back in with my parents; I gave up my job and my art in favour of a more temporary existence temping in offices. I pushed Seb away, convinced that since I wasn't the person he had signed up for, I would save him the awkwardness of breaking up with me. What else remained of who I'd been? Not my talent. I'd been obsessed with art and devoted to being an artist all my life. After the breakdown, I bowed out. I couldn't summon whatever had previously driven my making hands. It wasn't there any more. This more than anything seemed to prove that what had gone on was cataclysmic. What would I be now? Everything I had relied on to shape who I was had been obliterated.

I eventually came off the antipsychotics. They'd done the necessary. I had survived myself. They'd provided a bridge from terrified mania to a quieter but more manage-able state. I stuck with the antidepressants. I'd come to regard the medication as a safety measure. Like stabilisers. My brain, I felt, was not to be trusted. It couldn't possibly operate on its own, not without something to keep the madness from swelling up.

Recovery in the next few years felt like snakes and ladders. Months of mercifully unremarkable days and then dark hours and dark weeks, and once, a whole dark year without a moment's let-up to take a gulp of air or detect any hint of coming solace. Every time the mad, bad tide rolled in, I wept with familiar despair. *I will never be free of this* – this certainty lived in me.

Once you have stood on the precipice, it is hard to ever come back fully. You always know what the worst looks like. You know the texture and the taste of madness. And you always, always have a contingency. It's hard to admit this, but I hoarded medication for years. I promised myself that I would never be without an escape hatch. I never gave up my stock of sleeping pills until 2016, when I was prescribed strong medication to cope with severe pain after a complicated episiotomy. Deciding these would be even more effective and, more crucially, were in date, I replaced the old stash and carefully sealed the contingency plan away in my office in a hidden place that thrummed with shame.

As I got older, the stakes of my life had gotten higher and the potential fall-out of the contingency plan even more catastrophic. The boy who loved me was now the husband who loved me. My father was dead and my murder would leave my mother the sole survivor of our tiny, futile family tragedy. My body was home to two blond boys who hummed with life, each a bright, vibrating star who orbited me night and day. The contingency plan would murder them too.

But once you have touched the abyss and lived in it, a tiny part of you can't help but suspect that this abyss will one day be the end of you.

A thought dogs me still: that I have only ever outrun it momentarily, that still in the end it will be what finishes me. The thought comes with no shock or grief, only the same resigned inevitability that settled in my chest the day I considered my first contingency plan at twenty-two. In fact, the idea that it may not be entirely normal to keep a suicide plan in the back pocket in case of emergencies only struck me embarrassingly recently. In 2019, I was sharing in a recovery meeting. The subject of suicidal thoughts had been discussed and I offered up my contingency plan to the room. No one really answers you in these kinds of rooms. However, summoning words to articulate something that was previously only an unformed scrap in your mind can be as powerful as someone taking you by the shoulders and screaming in your face.

'It's not normal, is it?' I spoke to the silence. 'I should get rid of them, I guess. It's a bit like I'm not fully committing to life. Like all these years, I've just been toying with the idea of sticking around, just dipping a toe in. Keeping one foot on the dock.'

The room absorbed this and I left quickly after the meeting in case anyone tried to talk to me, I didn't quite manage the getaway. A woman intercepted me.

'Get rid of them, love. Bring them to the pharmacy.'

'I will,' I promised.

A few more weeks passed during which a small part of me – the part I need to manage, the ill part – made the case for keeping the pills. She harangued and pleaded. The pills are the escape hatch, though it does disturb me that the pills occupy the same building as my babies and their childish necessities. Lego and *Paw Patrol* toys, stuffed animals, puzzles and puppets all stored under the same roof as my grim needs.

In the office, I unlatch the dresser door and take the bag out of its box. I line all the pills up on my desk. It's the same desk on which I line up these words now. It is not enough to simply throw them away – they are volatile things. I crack each one open and dispose of the powder and capsules separately, so there is no danger of anyone swallowing my contingency plan whole. Then I line up these words as insurance. I am putting these words in this precise order to turn myself in, to confess. There is safety in committing this to the page you're holding. I need someone to know the extent of this thing, to make it public so that if I ever need, someone will intervene. These words are my new contingency plan.

HELL OF A TIME

When will I be better? How long until the keening thoughts will quiet? How many days have I fought this grinding doom? How many more?

In the months after my first breakdown at twenty-two, I was besieged with calculations of my misery. I was constantly trying to quantify this thing; trying to put a structure and framework on something that does not abide by any known logic.

I had two good days. I applied these words to the pages where I logged such information and held them like a prize. Two days of no thoughts of suicide. A sum that was both miraculous and sad. I would report such findings to Seb for his consideration.

'You are having good days,' he'd reassure me, holding me close.

On worse days, I would struggle to find a single hour untainted by the illness. *I had one good hour, which in eleven waking hours is actually not that bad. It's just under 10 per cent So, for 10 per cent of the day I felt almost normal.*

Of the people I'd found to help me through my illness – my psychiatrist, my psychologist, my friend Andrew who'd experienced similar – all had said the same thing regarding recovery: 'Time is the key.'

How fucking frustrating, I railed.

Time is beyond our control. Time has no physicality. It both does and doesn't exist. It's a human concept to give a sense of momentum to the otherwise meaningless chaos of life. There's no way to seek out time and apply it to my ills and I can't crank a lever to speed it up.

In dreams, time contorts and hours snap past. Because of my medication I already slept a considerable amount, but I couldn't sleep all the time. I did fantasise about convincing a doctor to induce a coma. I pictured a year-long rest and was convinced that this would give my brain a chance to relearn how not to be wild and demented anymore. Like in the *Valley of the Dolls*, when the protagonist Jennifer is prescribed the 'sleep cure' to lose weight. The idea was that she would down sleeping pills every time she felt hungry. I could down pills to eat up the time. In *My Year of Rest and Relaxation*, Ottessa Moshfegh's unnamed and nihilistic narrator induces a pharmaceutical hibernation to slog through the time of seemingly terminal apathy following the death of her not remotely cherished parents. I knew this plan wasn't actually practical, especially given most of the prescription meds in Moshfegh's book are invented, and so I wearily searched for other ways.

There's really only one instance when we can affect the passage of time in any tangible way and that is to have a really *good* time, then it slips by quicker than water through cupped hands. Time flies when you're having fun. And, let me tell you, time fucking *crawls* when you're having a nervous breakdown.

The only other practical way to wield any semblance of control over time, I decided, is to get lost, to ignore time so completely that it no longer applied. We can drop out of life, distance ourselves from the kinds of things governed by time, drift so far from its mechanics that it is irrelevant to us.

I read voraciously, almost desperately, in the months after the breakdown. This way I could be transported momentarily out of the painful present, and after which I could log a 'good hour', one relatively free from suicidal thoughts. I swam slow, deliberate lengths in the Markievicz pool before my temp job each day. One arm in front of the other, one breath pulled in and dispelled under the surface, before rising to grasp another breath. Another hour down. I essentially began to knit the seconds and minutes and hours of peace together.

I had to live very carefully. My old spontaneity and care-lessness was impossible after the precipice. But gradually

I began to imagine a future again, a fact that astounded me. I was putting things back in order. There was a bud of possibility. As good hours gradually became good days and then good weeks, I tentatively wondered at who I would be now that everything was different. I didn't mourn the artist I had thought I'd become; I accepted that that part of me was irredeemably over. But I did mourn the easy recklessness of the time before I realised I was so fragile. And I hated this new knowledge that my head was capable of such mad horror.

I went to South America and travelled for a few months with Seb and some of our closest friends. We made our way to New Zealand and I decided this would be the right place to hide and recuperate and learn a new way to live.

New Zealand is about as far from my home as you can be. People think of it as being beside Australia, when in fact it's a six-hour flight away. I liked the remoteness of New Zealand. It is verdant and tropical, volcanic and snow-capped, glacial and sulphuric all in the same two small islands. It's like a mushroom trip of geography. It was the perfect place to lose time.

I spent my years there seeking methodical, undemanding occupations to knit the moments together and force time along – to reach a point some way down the line when I could surely declare myself fully recovered.

I worked as a chef in tiny, rough-and-tumble kitchens where I learned how to dance the shouty, raging ballet of dinner service. Nothing makes you forget time like mains away on eight tables at once. I loved it. It was the perfect career for someone recovering from a nervous breakdown, or at least I thought so. Being on the line in a busy kitchen is the way to time travel: blink and frenetic hours of seething service have surged past. Cooking for dinner service is only ever about what has just happened, what is happening right now and what is just about to happen.

Everything is reduced down to basic steps that roll on indefinitely or until last orders are called. I have just seared the duck and it's gone in the oven; I'm dropping roasties in the fryer and I am just frying a portion of mushrooms for the next table's order. There can at this precise moment be no thought wasted on the table beyond that and the table beyond that. Nor can I ruminate on the table we sent five minutes ago. It is the most in-the-moment job on the planet. In fact moments in kitchens are not even moments but micros moments. If I pull that duck from the oven thirty seconds later than I should, it's wrecked: rare turned to medium, and another pan must go on the hob for more searing and a split-second reshuffle of tasks must happen to absorb the fuck-up.

Cheffing requires a certain mental agility – and not one I expected to possess in the aftermath of the breakdown – but I took to the practicality and immediacy of it like an exhausted person falls into bed at the end of a long day. The kitchen, with its emphasis on speed and rigorous attention to detail, dragged me from the thoughts that could still rear up. The pressure of the work distracted from the looping ill-logic. I couldn't agonise over whether I had gone mad or my life was a simulation or my arm was possessed in the kitchen. Or rather I could, but I still had to tend to about six other pressing tasks required to complete table six's order and not interrupt the flow of the kitchen. I also had to shout constant updates to my fellow chefs about where I was at with my components so that all our dishes could arrive to the pass in near-perfect synchronicity.

The cliché about chefs being quite mad and volatile people themselves is not cooked up from nothing. Anthony Bourdain, sadly similarly afflicted, said that chefs were the present-day outlaws and pirates of society, which was also my experience to a certain degree. There are few other workplaces in which you could announce you've gone mad from drugs and now can't quite believe that your memories of your life are real and be met with understanding. And good-hearted jokes.

The other method of time-travel I discovered in New Zealand was hiking. Moving through nature under your own steam is the antithesis of clock-watching. With the advent of train and car travel and eventually air travel, humans lost connection with distance, which arguably warped our concept of time, meaning we don't really understand it anymore. The digital age has further removed any physical connection between time and the human experience. We experience time as a loading bar rather than any physical action. When hiking, forward momentum is parcelled out in the change of light and distance and feet climbed, not time.

Hiking became a tangible strategy for restoring sanity. I walked for days through empty valleys and willed nature to heal me, which may seem like a ridiculously grandiose idea but is also a pretty sensible remedy. The author Mary Davis said, 'A walk in nature walks the soul back home.' Which definitely described what I was trying to do. In Emma Mitchell's book *The Wild Remedy*, she describes how she treats her chronic depression with nature, quoting the philosopher Søren Kierkegaard: 'Every day I walk myself into a state of well-being'. Obviously, it's not something that would've been possible during my worst times, but as I got better, this nature-bathing helped to put me back together. It's of course not a new idea: the Japanese even have a word for it – they call it Shinrin-yoku, or forest bathing. I think we are naturally inclined to seek out nature when we can. Beyond reducing stress, it tangibly affects our bodies too. Trees and plants release chemicals called phytoncides that boost our immune system.

Sometimes out on my own I would get a stab of fear at being so far from emergency intervention. What if I went mad out here? Then I would turn once more to the dense, empty green in front of me and mentally shrug. I went mad back there and I was still unreachable. I take my madness wherever I go. I came to accept this, and by walking off-grid, I had to learn to trust myself again. As Amy Liptrot wrote in her memoir of nature and recovery, *The Outrun*: 'I am filling the void with new knowledge and moments of beauty.'

I became as fluent in tramping as I'd once been in the world of drugs and narcotic escapism. My sleeping bag and tent, the site of my original breakdown, were now the most comforting place in the world to me. I hauled myself through the wide open. Hours and days passed and I was indifferent to the destination. I began to feel a tentative new normal creep in on me. This wasn't the person I thought I was. I had always been an indoor cat. Wine and spliffs and meandering conversation on the couch had been my default mode. And keeping up, of course, competing in the zealous game of achieving. I desperately wanted to succeed in college, keeping up with the life I was supposed to want. A first in college followed by a master's in a prestigious college in London. Accolades, recognition, an impressive life. I was only twenty-two and the concept that there are infinite ways to live was only just beginning to dawn on me.

Dropping out of life to become a chef in a remote and, as some would have seen it, provincial country was the exact opposite of what I was supposed to be doing. My family – people with interesting careers and impressive lives themselves – were baffled but not yet too worried. So far, it had just been months, not years, spent wandering.

Ask me now about the latest memes or best thing on TV and I will answer you without hesitation. But there's a notable and significant gap in my pop culture knowledge dating from the years 2007 to 2012. Popular TV shows, music and smartphones effectively bypassed me in those years. I stayed analogue for quite a bit longer than most. I didn't get a smartphone until 2015; I didn't have an Instagram account until 2016.

After two years in New Zealand, Seb and I decided to move to the French Alps. It was a continued bid to dodge life and accrue time, putting first months and then years between the breakdown and me. I no longer slavishly logged my periods of wellness. I existed outside of the traditional 9–5, Monday–Friday framework. I lived seasonally instead. We wanted to follow the winter from New Zealand to France where we would work in a ski resort and my affinity with the mountains continued. We snowboarded and worked hard. I learnt to 'skin', which is kind of like hiking on skis and was very effective, I found, for subduing any lingering madness that still presented occasionally. I spent long pre-dawn periods in cold, black, snow-covered forests on my touring skis, feeling unprecedented normality. And relief. I'd banked time that I was well enough to wean off my medication.

In the summers, with savings from our winter jobs, we dispensed even further with routine. One year we decided to live in tents and cycle around France and Northern

Spain for three months. The days followed a rhythm governed by miles and our appetites rather than any heed to minutes and hours. Our only grand plan was one dictated by money, which we eked out sparingly.

In May, we woke after a freezing night to snow on the ground in the Haute-Loire. We broke camp high in the valley and put on every item of clothing we had in our *panniers*, which was not much. With snow settling in the folds of our clothes we set off to the next village in search of a boulangerie and shelter. The cycle was desolate and beautiful in an apocalyptic kind of way. I vividly remember the figure of Seb just ahead of me, always on the cusp of being swallowed by the dense whiteness, but somehow remaining just visible. The fields on either side of this high mountain pass were luminous blue green in my immediate vicinity before falling away into the white-out and dissolving to nothing. It was the kind of lost I'd been reaching for since the breakdown. I felt safe on this dislocated path because it matched me. Other days on this trip were characterised by blinding heat and driving wind and rain. All were a pleasure. On the bikes, we experienced a panoply of humdrum sensations that were pure comfort to me. These weren't the trauma-manufactured hallucinatory feelings I'd been bombarded with for so long, just the pleasingly banal caress of weather and nature. The real. I was tired from cycling rather than obsessive thoughts; I was full of pastries instead of dread; I was short of breath from exertion not panic.

My family continued to be baffled by my indifference to 'getting on with life' as they saw it. We returned to Ireland occasionally for brief trips and they asked after my art. Did I not want to resume where I'd left off now that I was better? In our weeks at home, I could see my father was also beginning to drop out. While I was pursuing my lost years, he was succumbing to his. He hadn't yet been diagnosed as having early-onset Alzheimer's, but around this time it started as a slow prowl. My mother was strung between two ever-more absent loves, her daughter and her husband, but she tolerated it and, perhaps knowing what was ahead for us, she didn't beg me to stop getting lost and come home. She was so generous, so patient about my being gone, though she seemed confused at my rejection of niceties like hot showers and decent clothes.

The summer after the bikes was the summer of the van. In many ways the van-living was even more primitive than tents and cycling. I'd become fascinated by people living in alternative houses, converted shipping containers and retired red buses. I wanted to set up something similar in a remote field in Connemara. Seb insisted we aim for something a little less extreme, and so we bought our van off the internet. These were the days when people bought few things, much less important things, sight-unseen, from the internet.

We lived in the van on the edge of a car park in our deserted ski town beside the forest. I picked miniature

Alpine raspberries and rhubarb. I washed my hair infrequently with a water bottle.

We drove around Scotland, France, Germany, Denmark and Spain exploring and cycling the famous cols of the regions. In the evening, without TV or radio, we took turns reading while the other cooked dinner.

Reading a book with another person is a very particular shared moment. A communal dream, it reminded me of times when we'd taken mushrooms together and tripped in tandem in a tiny hotel room in Amsterdam. We'd shared the delirium, seeing panes of glass rippling like water under our touch, a child's pop-up book of space exploding in a cosmic ballet. A *folie à deux*. In a way, my subsequent madness had also been a shared one. Seb more or less came down the hole with me during my breakdown; he didn't feel the same fear and anguish, but he watched the ransacking take place. And when I was ready he stepped off the map with me and agreed to get lost together. We read Isabel Allende's *The House of the Spirits* and Evelyn Waugh's *Brideshead Revisited* – fitting as Seb is named after poor, doomed Sebastian Flyte.

When we did drive anywhere, we could charge the dinosaur laptop and treat ourselves to an episode of *The X Files*. Out in the world, the financial services had revealed themselves to be a disastrous collective *folie*. While people cried and died from the crush of debt and despair, we stayed hidden and lost and safe, setting ourselves the useless but eminently rewarding tasks of cycling up steep, almost vertical roads with miles and miles of switchbacks, then burning through brake pads on the descents. It felt like flying, more time put behind me as the miles racked up with each steady and comforting rotation.

I felt well. I felt like I could live this way forever. Simple appetites assuaged by simple meals. We ate crepes with mushrooms and Gruyère cheese. We concocted a pizza that was possible to make on our two-ring gas hob and grill – no oven required. We had no fridge, so meals demanded a certain amount of lateral thinking, perfect for me – I can happily pass all day planning my next meal and the one after that. By this time, our mid-twenties, Seb and I had fashioned a few homes together, almost always in vaguely impractical and often downright inhospitable nooks. In fact, we'd never lived anywhere remotely average together. Our first shared home was a crumbling coach house, complete with a beautiful, cast-iron bathtub under the eaves of the bedroom and no heating whatsoever. In New Zealand, we'd moved through a number of eccentric house-shares and then, after graduating from a tiny tent, we'd made a house in this small converted van.

Virtually everything we owned was in this van. The living space was about the size of two single beds and contained a small sink (no running water; we kept a large container of water in a cupboard underneath it), the stove and grill and a small square of 'counter space' that folded down over the sink for food prep. On the other side to the cooking area were cupboards that occupied the entire height of the van. At about 6ft tall, Seb was in a permanent stoop during this period. In these cupboards were the pantry of muesli, tinned vegetables and long-life milk, clothes, tools, books, and a stash of cash. More cash was secreted elsewhere. We did not have a bank account, instead we travelled with the total sum of our fortune (a few thousand earned during the working winters) hidden carefully around the van. Beyond the cupboards and kitchen, two bench seats ran to the back doors of the van, underneath which was more storage containing bedding and the lengths of MDF we used at night to bridge the benches and create a small bed. At eye level, a narrow ledge ran the length of the van on the side above the kitchen and continued above the bed. Along this we stored needful items like salt and pepper and torches along with various pointless but beloved tchotchkes, all secured with velcro so they wouldn't come loose when we were on the move. To this day, a music box containing a paper skeleton with hinged joints who dances when the music plays sits on a sideboard in our living room – with two pieces of velcro on the underside. It is battered from its years with us and now even more so because it's on the receiving end of the kind of violent love dispensed by small children, but whenever I look at it, I think of the distance and time we've travelled.

The van is where Seb suggested we get married the summer I was twenty-six. Well, not the van specifically, but a hammock that was tied between the van and a tree.

I returned to Ireland to live again aged twenty-seven. Seb and I got married and made yet another random but much-appreciated home in a set of bunk-beds in a room in my father-in-law's house while we tried to find our feet and catch up with the friends who by now had baffling things like careers and health insurance and hadn't embarked on a notions-filled, Kerouac fantasy.

We still have the hammock though not, sadly, the van – the van died somewhere just outside Athenry a couple of years later when our first baby was six months old. In the summers now, I hang the hammock in the garden of our very stationary, not-lost-but-very-firmly-located home in Dublin. I lie in its embrace and think about a younger us, swinging back and forth (it's a hammock made for two) and agreeing to get married and all the gamble and faith that entails.

The hammock swings like a pendulum and I think about how from that moment on, time shifted from something that I needed to ignore to something I needed to cherish. I agreed to get un-lost. I agreed to step back onto the grid. We did do one more winter in white, vast mountains where I pushed my touring skis through pristine untracked snow in the early hours before the day began and I took stock of what had been accomplished. I had weathered the breakdown. I still felt weird from time to time. I could still have bouts of the sickening terror. But mostly I knew I was real and I knew life was real which was, in fairness, progress.

By the time we returned to Ireland for good, five years had passed since my breakdown. And though it wasn't that long before another episode of mental illness, I still count this point as the end of my first recovery. As everyone had promised, it had taken time. It hadn't been linear and recovery continues, to this day, to feel like a series of fits, jolts and setbacks. I can bound forward and then plummet backwards, and the fear and frustration never wanes with each new episode. And I am sad to say that I have felt suicidal again in the intervening years.

However, in the first years after my initial breakdown I learned invaluable things about myself. In getting lost and un-lost, I now understood that nature and time both possess medicinal properties invisible to us until we desperately need them.

I had learned to manipulate time with the frenetic, exhilarating pressure of the kitchen. To dissolve it on lonely snowy stretches, to flee it clinging white-knuckled to a sliver of engineering with pedals and brakes powered only by me, to lose it along serene valley paths, to forget it driving my body up the steep ledges of jutting mountains and to savour it curled up with someone else in a shared dream.

PART 3
GORE AND MORE!

FAT AND BONES

I saw *EXERGIE – Butter Dance* in college in the early 2000s. It was a new piece of art then. Melati Suryodarmo enters a dimly lit space. She is Indonesian. She is beautiful. She is sturdy. She is fat. Or, at least, not *thin,* which to me right then is the same difference. She wears red high heels and a too-tight dress.

Before anything happens, I understand from her too-tight, too-short dress that she is desperate and grasping. I understand this in the way that like sees like. At twenty, I am also desperate and grasping. And fat – or at least powerfully convinced of it. Whatever.

In the centre of Suryodarmo's room is a slab of butter made up of twenty blocks: 20lbs of fat. In the weight-loss pro-gramme that I have danced around around for a few years at this point, they often congratulate a proudly diminishing woman with the block of butter analogy. 'You've lost a half a pound!' They are jubilant. 'That's half a block of butter!'

The enemy butter.

Suryodarmo steps on the butter and begins to dance, the sound of traditional Indonesian music accompanies her. She dances and falls, hitting the floor hard, rising, and continuously being on the verge of standing, slipping and falling in the butter. At times, on the floor she is greased and beached, and struggles to stand again. The spectacle becomes increasingly painful to even watch, never mind endure for Suryodarmo herself. Over and over, her legs fly from under her. She is slippery and so, so precarious in her sexy shoes.

After twenty minutes, Suryodarmo rises one last time, covered in butter, and leaves the space. The butter dance stays with me. It's nearly twenty years since I first saw it, but it lingers.

In the butter dance, I see all that is dangerous for a woman: appetite, sexiness, displaying our wants, displaying ourselves – all a dangerous and painful game. Sure, a man could dance on butter and fall over, but it would mean something different. It could read as slapstick and funny. But a woman slamming repeatedly into a hard surface can never be comedy for women. Our history, even on the tamest end, is littered with too much throwaway violence.

The year before I saw *EXERGIE*, a man followed me in Paris. He slammed my head into a wall. I don't at the time make any conscious connection between the repeated slamming of Suryodarmo on the greasy slab of ground and the colliding elements of my head, concrete, his hand, my hair, wrapped in his fist. I am twenty and not in the business of putting things together like this. I am twenty and events in my life seem to spin separately in space. My dad is sick. My body is a disappointment. I am starving for food and drugs and love. A man hurt me. Hair, hand, concrete. Another man hurt me. Screaming in my face. Another man hurt me. He dumps me saying he doesn't want me around anymore. At the time, the only connection I'm willing to see is me and my personal brand of wrongness. The events circle my wrong self and I am the root cause of them. I got in the way of the man's fist and the other man's wet, angry mouth. I was an embarrassment to the man who dumped me. I don't fit, I am wrong.

There are other (probably a few) reasons for the wrongness but one of the more innocuous ones I can date to an encounter the year I was nine. My mother and I were visiting a friend's house where they had a wonderful dress-up box. The kind a nine-year-old dreams of. I pulled a princess dress from the tangle of colourful silks and tulle. I was holding it up to my solid and surely sweet little nine-year-old body when the mother of the house announced that it was unlikely to fit me. I didn't quite know yet that

127

I was supposed to view this information as a core failing, that my appetite was being noted, that I was already perhaps too much. I merely wondered how she could tell such a thing without my *trying* it.

I gamely stepped into the dress still wearing my shorts and t-shirt. I pulled it over my bum and slipped my arms into the sleeves. It didn't close, but by my nine-year-old reckoning, it fit. It was on my body. Oddly this grown woman, apparently a committed pedant, was not content to let me just flounce around happily, and remain ignorant of my body's failure.

'See, I told you it wouldn't fit, it won't close. It's supposed to be suitable for ten- to twelve-year-olds!'

As if this performance of incredulity at my enormous nine-year-old body wasn't bad enough, the mother went on to say something quite astounding.

'Best take it off and maybe if you say "no" to puddings, next time you visit it will fit you.'

I wish I'd turned around and said, *Wow, fuck off, you psychopath*, but sadly I just absorbed the new information and allowed it to infiltrate every bite I allowed (or didn't allow) past my lips for the next two decades.

If you were born in the latter half of the twentieth century, then you will know that fat is the very worst thing. The worst thing to eat. The worst thing to be. In the nineties, everything was low-fat, fat-free, fat-burning, fat eradicating. In the nineties, we had heroin chic. Heroin. Chic.

If I hadn't witnessed it first-hand I would think it was some outrageous satire but no, fashion worshipped at an altar of undernourished children for several years before anyone apparently noticed how fucked-up that was. Growing up, to say you were on a diet in school was practically a badge of honour. Our 'diets' were usually Diet Coke and bananas so, ya know, like most diets, not a healthy approach.

Closer to home, Weight Watchers presided over the women in my family. The Illuminati of the fatties – an omnipotent force allocating points and punishment to unassuming foodstuffs and arbitrating a system of dubious gains and losses. In a tidy bit of patriarchal ingenuity, in the realm of fat they've left it to women to police each other's bodies, knowing that our drive to fulfil male ideals has nearly always overthrown our female solidarity.

Despite fat being historically mostly a woman's thing, the female body has always been a collective obsession and the aesthetic remit has always been to diminish it. I always thought of the Renaissance as having been a fat-loving utopia, but then I read cultural historian Dina Amlund's take on *Don Quixote*, considered the first modern novel. Quoted in conversation in Sofie Hagen's *Happy Fat*, Amlund describes Cervantes' overt fat-loathing. '[It's] about a man who lost his mind and travelled with his gullible, ill-smelling fat helper … It takes a fat person to fill that role of the unpleasant, unintelligent force.' Oof.

Sometimes Ruben is held up as the OG fat ally, but Ruben's women were really only vast when compared with depictions from any of the previous centuries or indeed those since. Plus, Rubens was just one guy. Along with so many other marginalised bodies, fat women were largely omitted from the canon of western art, while women of colour were egregiously white-washed. If they *were* depicted, as art historian Elizabeth McGrath detailed in her 1992 essay 'The Black Andromeda', it was more often than not in a servile role. The white-washing continues today: women of colour have been edged out of the very movements they founded. Author Stephanie Yeboah wrote in the *Guardian* of how slim, white women have co-opted the body positive movement to remedy issues of self-esteem over issues of discrimination:

> What we now had was a movement that celebrated aesthetically curvy, privileged bodies instead of bodies like my own, which ensures that the opinions, thoughts and perspectives of larger black women and women of colour are erased.

The ancient Greeks (the original arbitrators of taste) loved women, but they loved men more, and we have them to thank for the societal propensity to regard slim, white bodies as the aesthetic ideal because, surprise, surprise, the body considered to be ideal was white and male. Natch. Given that so much of women's status is connected to how we look, it's interesting and super irritating that pretty much from its inception, the system for attaining the physical ideal was rigged against women. Men naturally tend towards less body fat and more muscle.

Fat is, of course, essential to the female body. I know that denied of fat, certain functions will simply slow and stop, like menstruation. Meanwhile other new biological imperatives will awaken in attempt to protect the body even while it consumes itself – lanugo is hair the body grows to insulate itself when deprived of nourishment.

While the whole remit when I was growing up was to obliterate your abhorrent, all-too-human fat, ironically during those years it had as a substance actually became more visible. Cosmetic surgery meant it was possible to pull the fat right out of women and hold it up for examination. In *Fight Club*, the main characters steal the 'richest creamiest fat in the world', bags and bags of it from a liposuction clinic. Watching it I felt a shiver of shame on behalf of these fictional and unseen women whose inherent wrongness had been sucked out of them only for Brad Pitt and Edward Norton, both with bodies hewn to Greek perfection, to toss around callously. At one point one bag snags on barbed wire, spilling forth the sloppy mess of female humiliation. Somehow it was my humiliation too.

'Tyler sold his soap to department stores at $20 a bar,' the narrator explains. 'Lord knows what they charged. It was beautiful. We were selling rich women their own fat asses back to them.'

The action was cast as a rebellion against capitalism, while the casual loathing of women went unnoticed.

The pale and jagged Marla of the sunken eyes sent another subtle message in *Fight Club*: being a strong-willed woman is synonymous with a certain unhinged quality. They were beautiful outliers. And to be one of these erratic, complex, strong-willed women you had to be really thin. When I was growing up these were the only complex women we ever saw. Think Courtney Love. Think the jutting hips of Elizabeth Wurtzel on the cover of her 1994 memoir, *Prozac Nation*, the starved and doomed girls of *Girl, Interrupted*, the endlessly surveyed body of Fiona Apple who was either ethereal and beautiful or gaunt and worrisome – certainly profiles of the time rarely make it to the end without picking over her body in some respect.

I loved these women for pushing against the epidemic of compliant women and silent women in mainstream culture. But I also accepted that to be interesting, I must be like them and to be like them, I must be less. They were only allowed to push because, despite their rebellion, they also participated in the economy of hotness. They could subvert it slightly with their gutsy works of art, but should they stray too far from the ideal, they could shout and rage all they wanted, no one would listen to them. They would be erased.

Refusing beauty was a defiant act. In the early nineties, a French artist called Orlan upturned the beauty contract using the very methods becoming ever more available to women with the financial means. It was a feminist appropriation of the beauty industry to undermine the impossible-to-attainable standards that drove it. Orlan, an objectively very attractive woman, set about erasing her beauty. She chronicled the numerous cosmetic procedures this required in her work. She wanted to sculpt herself to resemble the great women of art history. With scalpel and stitches, she made herself a patchwork: the mouth of Europa by François Boucher, the chin of Botticelli's Venus, and Mona Lisa's slightly jutting brow using implants usually used to augment cheekbones. She saw her work as a critique of the male gaze and the role of women in Western art – nude, observed and passive. With her plastic surgeries, her aim was never to be conventionally beautiful but to discard the blueprint and create herself.

'It's a critique of beauty and a critique of cosmetic surgery. I have given my body to art.' She told the *New York Times* in 1993 while she was still in the middle of what ultimately became a ten-year extended performance, *The Reincarnation of Saint-ORLAN*.

To me, what's amazing even beyond Orlan's commitment to her work is the fact that she managed to convince cosmetic surgeons – who all waived their fees – to do it. Her slew of radical surgeries suggests a level of body autonomy not usually afforded to women. As recently as 2019, women were still fighting doctors to perform tubal ligation with the condescending reason being that they were too young (often at twenty-seven and older) to be able to make such a decision. One woman was told the procedure was reserved for women in their thirties or forties who already had at least two children. Another, when she finally convinced her doctor to give her the tubal ligation, had to bring her husband in with her to give his 'consent'. I was not required to accompany my husband to his vasectomy to give *my* blessing.

Orlan made an elaborate ritual of many of her surgeries, neatly exposing the sacrificial role of women when it comes to beauty standards. Among the artefacts arranged in the (operating) theatre where she performs her brutal transformations are jars of fat previously removed from her body.

This rejection of beauty is something I wish was courageous enough to do. Even writing this piece, I feel I'm being duplicitous by not mentioning that I am thinking a lot about my own body at the moment. Free of my last baby, the taut belly is deflated and my flesh and fat pools on the mattress when I lie on my side at night. I pull at my fat and wish that obliterating it didn't tempt me so much. But how could it not? When I think of those formative years, I see myself and my friends as witnesses to an apocalypse played out on TV, in the movies and in the magazines.

Armies of beleaguered and hungry women played the role of everyone we ever saw. They were the TV doctors, the TV lawyers, the TV mothers and the TV girlfriends. Thin white able-bodied women were the protagonists of every situation. If a fat woman or woman of colour appeared it was only ever in the context of a best friend – a repository for the woes of the main character. Her one storyline, if she got one, was to be troubled by her weight. It decimated my self-esteem and confidence. It condemned women and it has been fatal. While eating disorders are not solely caused by this, it is the only illness whose devastating effects you will be commended for, at least at the disease's onset.

'You're looking great – have you lost weight?'

I've always had an obsession with horror. Throughout my teens I watched all the biggies: *The Exorcist*, on repeat, *Screams 1, 2* and *3*, and my favourite, the most demented of the lot, *The Texas Chainsaw Massacre*. Being a horror fan back then was something a little peripheral, a bit underground compared to prime-time telly. However, I barely noticed that the single biggest horror show at that time was available right there on prime time; it was gory, exploitative and tragic. And I ate it up. I am talking about *The Swan*, of course.

It was, as some said at the time, reality TV's lowest moment, but I couldn't look away. It was a spectacle of normalised violence. For anyone lucky enough to have escaped *The Swan*, here's the gist: contestants were 'ugly' women who were brought on the show to transform into a swan. The finalist each week would ultimately enter a pageant to compete to be the overall winner.

The transformation claimed to be a holistic, 360° approach, taking time to help the women address their self-esteem issues, though whatever therapy took place also went hand-in-hand with a physical overhaul that bordered on dismemberment.

I watched *The Swan* religiously and I never gave it any critical consideration whatsoever. LOL of course I didn't, I was nineteen and envious of the contestants and the life-changing transformation they were undergoing. However, I also knew that I wouldn't have the guts to undergo such procedures. It didn't occur to me that perhaps it was not something that any woman should be summoning the guts to endure. I just watched the women in bandages crying down the phone to their families after a full-body refurbishment and understood that changing and improving our bodies – by counting calories or braving incisions – was something that women did and men did not (obviously this has changed since). The show's experts weighed in from time to time, commending the women's resilience and regularly remarking that so many procedures were almost *never* carried out in such a short space of time. The procedures were a manual remodelling: the women's noses were broken, their jaws realigned, their breasts sliced and stuffed and restitched.

And then of course there was the fat. Fat was sucked from buttocks, hips, thighs and abdomen and sometimes the chin, neck, upper arms, breasts, knees, calves or ankles too. Hardly an inch of the body escaped this extraction.

Post-op, the women were bruised and battered, and shaken. If I had been older, I think this show would've scared me more than *The Texas Chainsaw Massacre* – it was chilling, revealing such an on-the-nose truth about being a woman in the world. How we must be upgraded and enhanced in order to matter. It is some relief to know that at the time critics were roundly disgusted by the show. They lamented the normalisation of cosmetic surgery and the simplistic message that financial and relationship problems could be remedied by physical transformation.

However, sometimes I think the criticism is condescending to these women who were surely not so naive as to think their problems would disappear with the modifications. Perhaps what they really wanted was just to move through the world more easily. Jennifer Pozner described it as 'the most sadistic reality series of the decade' in her book *Reality Bites Back*, but it was only as sadistic as the culture that produced it. We are obsessed with the Before and After of women. It's always implied that there is a destination to reach, a state of perfection to achieve before our lives can commence. Anyway, I wasn't reading feminist critical theory at nineteen. I was grabbing my fat and getting the message. That message was everywhere, albeit in more subtle ways than in *The Swan*. To look back on the era, there were five fat women allowed on TV: Dawn

French, Jo Brand, Miss Piggy, Rosanne and Oprah (who was only fat occasionally). There were also a few women that were *sold* to us as 'fat' who were objectively not fat, like Sophie Dahl or Renée Zellweger in *Bridget Jones' Diary*.

Post op, the women of *the Swan* were mummified awaiting their reincarnation; their fat sat in vats while they lay bandaged on the bed. It reminded me of a construction site. In the weeks after the operations, girdles and support garments acted like scaffolding holding their bodies in position and keeping them from spilling their organs and viscera.

In college, maybe in an attempt to make peace with fat, I was briefly preoccupied with fat in my work, of course I was. Fat to me occupied a compelling liminal space – the no-man's-land between smooth, yielding skin and the bones and organs and muscles below. Seen yet unseen, persistently and roundly loathed. I got the idea of liberating the fat. I wanted people to touch it. So at twenty-one, I would trawl butchers for the fat of animals and create objects rendered in tallow. The process itself was a slog. Unwittingly, I was mirroring the process from *Fight Club*. The animal fat needed to be boiled for hours and produced a heavy atmosphere. The smell was offensive. The tallow, however, was perfect: the finish smooth and pristine like the marble bodies I drew in museums, but much closer to life. The marble bodies were beautiful but contained, but these objects rendered in fat had something else. For starters they responded to touch – anyone could leave a mark. The tallow had a truer connection to the body than the marble. It was an in-joke for me, proof that the unassuming fat held up for our derision and disgust in *The Swan* and *Fight Club* could be beautiful and not an admittance of some obscure failure on my part.

For me and every other devoted eater, the villainous fat in cooking is almost elemental. It's essential to imbuing everything with a compelling flavour; it drives the impulse to dip a potato into the sticky roast chicken tray. It is the smearing of butter and its close relative, cream, that lends decadence to otherwise pretty workaday scones and cakes. In recent years, the fat taste has come to be accepted as the sixth taste sense. It is considered repellent in complete isolation but add something – anything! – and my god it's good.

My butter consumption has always been monitored by my mother. She doesn't approve – I think she would genuinely rather stumble upon me cradling a crack pipe than gorging on butter. Butter is a food group unto itself for me and wherein once it was the enemy, it has now come to represent a micro rebellion.

Butter was the battlefield of a different kind of revolt for Dorothy Wordsworth, sister and caretaker of William. She was also an unlikely forerunner to Orlan's rejection of aesthetic obedience. When Wordsworth got married, Dorothy was devastated. Overnight she was divested of her duties to cook and feed and accompany him on his walks. Her journals describe the fresh bread and butter and tarts of buttery pastry and fatty chops she had placed before him for many years, now no longer required. From her writing, it sounds like on his wedding day she was struck down with delirium. In bed the night before, she has tossed with anguish, apparently wearing the wedding ring William would be presenting to his wife. A little unusual, you'll agree. She gave it over in the morning, though it sounds like it was grudging. After Dorothy became ill with dementia in later life, she went to live with the William and his wife and family during which time Dorothy seems to have begun a passive revolution of sorts. She grew enormous. She was placed in a room in the house and rarely moved; if she did she needed the support of two others. She demanded food, constantly complaining of a hollow feeling. Me too, hun, me too.

She became the needy centre of the household, reversing her lifelong role as carer and disrupting the family that she surely resented. I'm not saying it was all one big revenge-fuelled long game, but surely she must've enjoyed wresting back William's attention to some extent. According to food historian Laura Shapiro, William fought desperately with her about food. He wrote to a friend: 'She has a great craving for oatmeal porridge – principally for the sake of the butter that she eats along with it.' Her fatness, it seemed, was a calamity, though Shapiro argues that Dorothy's decline had 'moments of triumph'. In her book *What She Ate*, which tells the stories of six notable women through their food, she describes 'Dorothy in her chair, round and imperious as royalty, demanding porridge so that she could eat the butter'. A moment of protest, or vengeance, or just simple satisfaction.

So much of my favourite food has acquired enemy status. I've always had a subconscious manifesto of the rights and wrongs of food. Before the clean eating movement provided such an on-the-nose system for cataloguing the clean and the dirty, the good and the bad, I knew in my fat and bones what food was safe and not safe to eat. Salad was a powerful choice: it reflected well on me and my femininity. Declaring I was full was the ultimate statement. Denying my appetite was the best way I knew how to impress my mother and other women. I understood it as a kind of Venn diagram of acceptable states of appetite. You can be hungry, so long as you are thin. The 'cool girl eating junk food' trope commends thin women for being real and refreshingly un-neurotic when they eat pizza.

The inventory of my food has kept me neatly preoccupied with my body and annexed a frankly massive portion of my brain. When I first moved in with my husband, I became aware of just how much time and mental energy I willingly gave over to this eating business. I edged around different foods like I was navigating a minefield. I weighed and counted and sorted and agonised and forensically catalogued while he simply ate. It was eye opening. There was an ocean of useless knowledge of food and its calorific value and corresponding social currency flooding the space where I could be thinking about me and my life and my desires.

He simply ate. I put food in my mouth with a deranged trifecta of trepidation, guilt and longing, while he simply ate. While I chose salad at dinner to tell a complex – not to mention irrelevant – story about myself (that I was above such base obsessions as carbs), he chose what he wanted most in that moment. And just fucking ate it.

A friend told me about the ortolan, a tiny French songbird considered to be a forbidden culinary delicacy, illegal since 1999. The ortolan is kept in darkness for weeks being force-fed, before it is drowned in Armagnac. It's then plucked and roasted, before the eater lowers it feet-first into their mouth and devours it whole. It's said that as one crunches through the bird's skeleton, the tiny bones often nick the gums, adding blood to the mix – a sort of seasoning for the experience. Larger bones are spat out. The act apparently arouses such pleasure and such shame that those who perform it do so with their heads covered with their napkin so as to hide the heinous act of gluttony from god.

'It sounds like a woman just eating … fucking anything.' I comment grimly.

I still grapple, applying so much meaning and morality that at times it literally feels like my husband is eating different food from me. That my food, food in the hands of a woman, is a poison to be carefully, oh so carefully, administered.

When women aren't small and beautiful, they are often punished with the swift removal of their femininity and even humanity. Unlovely women are called men or dogs, and seem to illicit genuine rage from some quarters. What are we for if not providing aesthetic satisfaction for others? Once when I was a teenager walking down the street a group of older boys were walking behind me. Seeing my long white-blonde hair, one of them sang, 'Turn around honey … let us see your face.'

I had lovely hair, which to my mind only served to compound the very noticeably unlovely rest of me. Still, I was thrilled, though a little apprehensive. I did glance back in their direction, which prompted gales of laughter and the unforgettable words, 'Oops, never mind – you're a dog!'

Feeling ugly as a teenager seems to be a fairly universal experience, but I felt the fact of my ugliness as tangibly as a limb. Boys at school echoed the 'dog' sentiments of the crowd above and the phrase 'ugly' felt as though it had been invented for me personally, an astounding new level of self-absorption, if I do say so myself. I railed at the injustice of being a teenage girl. *It doesn't matter for boys. They're allowed to be fat or ugly and no one cares.*

Even the micro slights cause erosion: *She has a lovely face. She could be so pretty.*

She just needs to change is all we hear.

At times, my body has behaved, but only because I starved it into submission. On my wedding day, I was tiny. Depressingly, I bought wholesale into the seemingly non-negotiable idea that whoever I may have been before this wedding, I must shed at least two stone of that person in order to participate. For weddings, men must get a suit and women must get a thigh gap and pronounced clavicles.

On the day, I was 10 stone: 140 pounds or 140 blocks of butter. I hadn't been 10 stone since I was ten years old, but in the run-up to this day where I was the centrepiece, I switched gears and aggressively ate virtually nothing. Apparently, at 5′8″, I was at my ideal weight. I'd never been the ideal anything and couldn't get over the near-constant validation of this life in a smaller body. It was intoxicating. More satisfying than eating ever was, I immediately decided. I'd never before been praised for doing anything as much as I was praised for not eating. Though not everyone was so ardent.

'I can see your bones,' Seb said flatly as I got dressed in the morning. My husband didn't seem as pleased, but then he wasn't high off the fumes of finally being worthy.

'Oh it's not that bad …' I was thrilled. I was now a thin person with all the attendant complaints that thin people enjoyed. I was constantly cold, which for some reason was deeply satisfying. I needed a pillow between my knees at night to prevent the bones from rubbing uncomfortably. I was truly, madly fascinated by the butterfly of fine bones etched across my chest and each notch of vertebrae that appeared down the centre of my back was a new level of rightness attained.

The hunger game was one of dubious methods and shallow rewards. I aimed to eat no more than 1200 calories a day, which is about what is recommended for a toddler. On a really good day, 1000 calories would do me. I achieved an almost savant-like talent for addition and subtraction, adding calories and devising ever more inventive ways to subtract fat, not to mention *flavour*, from the meagre meals I deigned to ingest.

I could plainly see that, despite my husband's concern, my being thin added to my market value. I attracted attention as a thin woman that I didn't in my heavier body. As a really thin woman, I could participate in the system that had previously been closed to me.

I'd go to bed high off the deprivation. I began to associate the feeling of hunger with a feeling of boundless success. In the mornings, I'd hold out on eating until lunchtime, drinking coffee to stave off pangs from my body. In all this, however, I never saw it as enough. I never felt I'd arrived at my destination. I never felt thin in the moment, only after months would I look back on photographs and spot my bones rising like a wreckage to the surface of my flesh.

I wonder if I was drifting into an eating disorder around this time. Certainly I was in an unhealthy cycle of obsession, but really, was it any different from so many other women's baseline state of denying our longing for fat? Our enduring wish for bones and praise?

We know the pursuit of beauty has always been dangerous for women. In the 1800s, we cheerfully poisoned ourselves with lead and arsenic in make-up products; in the 1900s we deformed our rib cages and misaligned our spines with corsets; and in the twentieth century, *à la* The Swans, we've casually sliced and injected our way to the uncanny beauty of late capitalism.

The narrative on the magazine rack has subtly altered though – now nobody wants to admit to *trying* to be thin (let's shelve for a moment the rightness, wrongness or sheer tediousness of wanting to be thin). Now a celebrity must be 'strong', not skinny, which is all very admirable but it seems disingenuous to pretend that's what it's all about.

Author Lindy West highlighted this exhausting paradox in an essay in *Self Magazine*:

> We're supposed to be hot in all the old ways while appearing liberated in the new ones. We're expected to devote ourselves to weight loss as much as our mothers and grandmothers did, while at the same time orchestrating

an elaborate cover-up: this modern weight loss is always
a coincidence, a by-product of our 'wellness practice', an
incidental surprise.

The way we talk about our bodies is changing, but the shift
feels semantic. Many of us are still striving to minimise
ourselves. At this very moment, in fact, I am not eating
sugar. I don't talk about it unless asked and even then I
am coy. I'm claiming to be *feeling* amazing, pretending it
is nothing whatsoever to do with how I look. I'm disappointed in myself. I want to be above this. I want to shed
the fear of fat, but do I still want to shed the fat more?

The weight-loss industry has had to undertake a mass
rebrand with many diets now claiming empowerment as
their main aim rather than weight loss. Whatever it takes
for us to swallow it, right? And stay riveted to tracking
our slide up and down the scale. We cannot simply be, we
must always be en route to a better self: as Leslie Jamison
says in *The Empathy Exams*, women are a 'horizon of antic-
ipation'. We're always under construction.

When I was an artist, I wanted to make work about the
dilemma of being a woman. I created sculptures designed
to extend and contort the body. I captured performances
of these works, with either myself or a model wearing the
pieces. In one, I sewed elaborate, almost prosthesis-like
elements into a costume, so that the wearer looked like
an overstuffed antique armchair, albeit one that could

crawl around and had a head. In another piece, I made an enormous horn-like structure that was covered in fabric, hung in space, and measured over 8ft long. A model was suspended from the ceiling parallel to the floor in a harness and laced into the horn at its narrowest end, just like a dress. She could not move – the horn, though it elongated her in a fashion, also devoured her – and yes, I love *Little Shop of Horrors*. She was both extended and confined by the dress, beautiful but stymied.

Now in the age of digital beauty, technology has given us the means to re-sculpt our own appearance, echoing my attempts to extend myself and other women. It's surprisingly democratic in a way – no longer is cosmetic alteration the sole preserve of the rich. However the casual virtual reincarnation of everyone's online selves is unnerving. It would almost make you miss the vats of fat. Almost. At least that was honest self-mutilation as opposed to the stealth variety that pervades our social media feed.

When I was a fat-collecting, fat-boiling artist, I fell in love with the painter Jenny Saville. Her vast, blotchy, oozing, soft, pink and fleshy fat women were, for me, like gazing into a mirror. I was reflected in Saville's canvas both in terms of her, a woman, being the author of the work, and in the affinity I felt with her women. They were women whose underwear cut into their unruly, fat bodies. They bore marks where tools of abuse cut into their unruly, fat bodies too.

I didn't get to see a Saville in the flesh until years later in the Tate Britain. I never understood the mammoth scale until I saw one. It was powerful: a woman artist training the female gaze on the kind of woman largely ousted from the aesthetic narrative, and for that rendering to be so epic in proportion. The painting covered an entire wall, floor to ceiling. Saville's raw fat woman stared down from the canvas and threatened to engulf everyone who gazed back.

Carved into the paint of one of Saville's paintings is part of a text from Belgian-born feminist writer Luce Irigaray. The words are scrawled in mirror image, maybe intended more for the woman in the painting than the viewer, who is forced to read it backwards:

> If we continue to speak in this sameness – speak as men
> have spoken for centuries, we will fail each other. Again,
> words will pass through our bodies, above our heads –
> disappear, make us disappear.

But here I am, still feverishly policing myself from time to time. A compulsive little disappearing act of my own. I want to be better than this but it's hard to shake the hangover that fat is the very worst thing. The worst thing to eat, and the worst thing to be.

Sometimes during periods when my relationship with food is amicable and I am happily revelling in the pleasures of eating, I will still catch myself hiding how much butter I am putting on anything. When Seb butters my toast I slip back to the kitchen to re-butter it. If I'm eating roast potatoes in the presence of my mother, I automatically temper how much butter I put on them. Ideally, if I was on my own, I wouldn't be putting butter *on* them at all, rather I'd be scooping the butter up from its dish *with* them, treating the butter like a dip. To do this in front of her would ruin it – her open disgust would, in an instant, stir the dormant disgust I carry with me about my body.

But why should we disappear? We are hungry. We need fat. Why punish ourselves with any further deprivation when there is butter in the world?

CRAVING

I had been pregnant for about six months when an unruly obsession set in. I wanted something that was virtually impossible to have. Blood. For the first few days of the lust, I felt odd about admitting it. It seemed like such a vaudeville cartoony kind of pregnancy craving. Actual blood. Embarrassing really. Like my teen flirtation with being a goth had been somehow re-activated. There was a disappointingly banal reason behind the craving. I was anaemic. But however banal the reason, it didn't make the sensation any less strange. And it was strange. Craving, yearning, salivating for a drink of blood.

I began to hunt for something, anything that might answer my body's call for blood. Before you ask, as everyone did at the time, no, a rare steak was too insipid. The fatty, rusty juices were Ribena to wine in terms of what I wanted.

Each day was accompanied by this offensive hunger, and what emerged was that the urge for blood was about more than merely taste and satisfying the depletion of iron in my body. It was about texture. It was about the perfect temperature. It was about a certain fantasy. While I would have accepted a pint of blood, what I really wanted was to drink from the source. I wanted an elegant sheet of blood to fall from a precise and neat slit and cascade over me. In the fantasy, it was a person whose neck I crouched beneath, ready to lap at the thick and, more importantly, warm wellspring. An animal was just not very appetising.

It was such a wrong thing to want. It occurred to me that the position of frantic desire is always going to be wrong. The wrongness is the oxygen to the inferno. The wrongness intensifies the need. The wrongness makes it interesting. It makes it irresistible.

I felt like I was getting an insight into the plight of the psychopaths and the murderers and the cannibals. What it's like to want the unwantable.

In *Apocalypse Culture* by Adam Parfrey, there is an interview by Jim Morton with Karen Greenlee, another woman who wanted the unwantable. Karen was a necrophiliac. In all my research of the macabre, Greenlee is a trailblazer. And my research has been considerable. I've managed to parlay this hobby into a bit of a full-time job.

For more than two years my friends Jen O'Dwyer, Cassie Delaney and I have come together every week to tell each other horrific stories: weird, violent, sad, funny, gross and morbid ones for our podcast *The Creep Dive*. And while we've talked about plenty of male necrophiliacs, I hadn't ever come across any female necrophiliacs until I read about Karen. Men seemed a lot more prolific in this area. Is there something in the fact that men dominating women is the acceptable narrative around sex? Are these female necrophiliacs just trying to be a bit more take charge in their sexual encounters?

Ok but jokes aside, poor Karen did appear to be deeply conflicted about her urges. She worked in a mortuary and in a note she wrote before attempting to overdose on codeine, she admitted to 'amorous episodes' with between twenty and forty dead men. This letter was something of a lament:

> Why do I do it? Why? Why? Fear of love, relationships. No romance ever hurt like this … It's the pits. I'm a morgue rat. This is my rathole, perhaps my grave.

Karen survived and was sentenced to eleven days in jail and a $255 fine (so specific).

In her later interview, Karen seems more defiant and ready to defend her appetites. When questioned on the mechanics of the thing, she explains:

> The most sensitive part of a woman is the front area … and that is what needs to be stimulated. Besides there

are different aspects of sexual expression: touchy-feely, 69, even holding hands. That body is just lying there, but it has what it takes to make me happy. The cold, the aura of death, the smell of death, the funereal surroundings, it all contributes ... there is also this attraction to blood. When you're on top of a body it tends to purge blood out of its mouth, while you're making passionate love... You'd have to be there I guess.

Indeed.

I know this description should be roundly dissuading me from wanting the pesky unwantable, but I can't help it. I want this blood on a molecular level. It's a vile urge that doesn't so much belong to me as propels me. I'm possessed. I'm just the channel it moves through. And would it satisfy me? Is it safe? I look it up and apparently no, not really. A few teaspoons of blood won't do us any harm but ingesting more is toxic, causing an iron overdose that we are not physiologically equipped for. So disappointing, as I sense if I get my hands on any blood, it will be moreish. A few teaspoons will not do. I don't want parsimonious sips of blood. I want to guzzle it.

I keep tripping up on the aesthetics of the thing. It's so 'art school' of me to be fixating on blood. I'm mortified by this craving. It's like Hermann Nitsch's tantruming pieces from the sixties. His flinging around of blood and carcasses in the gallery made me cringe in college, just like the thought of my kneeling pregnant under a wound makes me cringe now. It all seems so over the top.

Male artists seem to dabble in blood for the shouty splash of novelty. Whereas for women it's not novel – we are more matter-of-fact about blood. We're dealing in it in a much more ho-hum capacity. Blood must be taken care of. It's just an act of personal management.

I push the oozing steaks aside and venture further, to the internet of course.

I think, ethically speaking, I must at least try my own blood first. If that quells the appetite, then there'll be no need for further letting. I would need a dodgy phlebotomist. But unfortunately there's just nothing intriguing about my own blood. The idea of drinking my own is about as enticing as masturbating. It would maybe scratch the itch of the craving but it wouldn't satisfy me in any significant way.

I catch myself cataloguing friends, identifying whose blood I'd most like to have. There's no obvious criteria among my top three. They are different from each other in every way possible except that they are all women. Delicious women.

Online I explore consensual vampirism and wonder if I could possibly convince any of my friends to give me some blood. There's precedent for it. In the Real Vampire communities online, they'd be called donors. People who essentially buddy up with the vampires or 'Sangs' as they're sometimes called, short for 'sanguinarians'. One ethnographer, John Edgar Browning, while studying the Sang community, actually submitted to a feeding. He allowed an incision to be made in his back for a subject of his research to feed from. Browning suggests that there could be thousands of practising vampires in most major cities and I am momentarily buoyed by the thought. I'll make contact with one, find a donor to feed on. Then again, do I want stranger blood? The blood of my friends seems just that bit more appealing.

I eventually decided that it would be wrong of me to even ask: these friends are all mothers. The demands on them are too much already. They're being drained at every turn. They don't need creepy me slinking around, angling for blood.

Craving blood in pregnancy is not as common as craving what are, to my mind, far stranger things like coal, soap and paper. Yet despite the lack of recognition among articles about pregnancy online, I am sanguine (*ba-dum tss*) about my urge to drink blood. There is a whole tradition of medicine I can lean on to bolster my conviction that my blood thirst does not mean I'm a disgusting deviant; I'm actually in good company. For a few hundred years, spanning the fifteenth, sixteenth and seventeenth centuries, consuming humans was in vogue among European royalty, scientists and even priests. They branded it well, calling the practise 'corpse medicine' or 'medicinal cannibalism', which lends a certain legitimacy. Is that how I could pitch it to my friends? 'May I medicinally cannibalise you, please?'

In 1492, in a pretty on-brand move, a pope – Pope Innocent VIII – drank the blood of three young boys on his deathbed in an attempt to stave off the end. A few hundred years later, England's King Charles II had a personal remedy of alcohol infused with bits of human skull, which became known as 'The King's Drops'. The skulls in question were often Irish and procured by nefarious means.

'Medicine' does seem a generous term for this craze; the treatments were, at times, amusingly literal. There seemed to be a distinct trend of like-for-like remedies. Powdered skull was recommended for head ailments, blood for infections of the blood. Human fat was rubbed into surface wounds. Compounds of skull, fat and blood were even sold in apothecaries. In Germany, poorer people who couldn't afford over-the-counter human remains could instead go to executions with a cup and simply stand underneath the platform where the executioner was swinging his sword and capture the condemned man's blood once he was beheaded. This was apparently a cure for epilepsy.

As I toyed with the idea of finding a willing donor, I was feeling more and more certain that a donor or 'black swan', as they're also known, would probably not quite do the trick. Most contemporary vampires are almost disappointingly clinical in the extraction and consumption of blood. For many of them it is simply serving what they perceive to be a physiological lack. They often retrieve the blood with lancets – there's no seductive sheet of blood I can crouch under. There is rigorous medical testing required of both parties, contracts and even a Donor Bill of Rights are involved. Plus, most problematic for me, they are deeply scathing of what they call 'lifestylers', someone merely dabbling. A bloody flirt.

In my research, I come across clinical vampirism, a psychological obsession with drinking blood. According to one of the rare studies of the disorder:

> Clinical vampirism is named after the mythical vampire, and is a recognisable, although rare, clinical entity characterized by periodic compulsive blood-drinking, affinity with the dead and uncertain identity. It is hypothetically the expression of an inherited archaic myth, the act of taking blood being a ritual that gives temporary relief.

It's also sometimes called Renfield's syndrome, though it's not recognised in much medical literature and is usually rejected as a real condition by psychiatrists. The supposedly-not-really-a-thing syndrome got its name from the character of Renfield in Bram Stoker's *Dracula*. With Stoker's first introduction of him, I feel an immediate affinity with poor doomed Renfield – a resident in an insane asylum:

> R.M. Renfield, age 59. Sanguine temperament, great physical strength, morbidly excitable, periods of gloom, ending in some fixed idea which I cannot make out.

It me! I thought. Morbidly excitable, periods of gloom, baffling fixations. Check, check, check. Really apart from the age and physical strength, Renfield and I are one and the same. Though Renfield eats birds and my current pash for blood means I have more in common with Stoker's Dracula than with Renfield. Like the reptilian count, I long to be 'gorged with blood' and lie 'like a filthy leech, exhausted with (my) repletion'. Though Renfield does fall under the influence of Dracula, and maybe this is what this hunger is.

The whole vampire thing, while new, comes as absolutely no surprise to anyone I tell about it. I have what could be classed as a pathological enthusiasm for the macabre, so my endless googling of 'drink blood okay?' and 'where can get blood?' isn't going to ruin my Google search history. Or rather it won't ruin it any more than two years of co-hosting *The Creep Dive*, a podcast about ickiness in all its forms, already has.

Blood-sucking has always been connected with consuming the victim's energy to replenish one's own. Therefore perhaps craving blood doesn't seem so odd in the context of the interloper baby siphoning off every scrap of nutrients and energy through the placenta.

Babies in the womb don't exactly have our blood running through their veins, but their blood does infiltrate ours by way of cells that can be found in the mother's bloodstream for years after giving birth.

My own blood was wary of the baby from the get-go. I'm rhesus negative, meaning should the baby's blood not match my own, and if any of it should cross the placenta, my body would treat it as a foreign entity and attack. My god, pregnancy is so weird. The side effects run from the irritating to the painful to the bizarre. And the annoying thing about pregnancy is that you can take your ailments to any doctor and mostly they'll just shrug and put it down to pregnancy.

Sometimes though, you'll regret them taking you seriously as the investigation can be quite ad hoc, often with a side of discomfort and mild humiliation. I still shudder at the cough test, a procedure I was treated to that involved people (medical professionals I hope) looking 'up' me to see if amniotic fluid was leaking. It seems a bit lo-fi, doesn't it? I feel like if the men were doing pregnancy they'd get a cool laser or body-scanning machine for this stuff.

If men did pregnancy, all those films about heroic space travel and war would never have been made and instead every action movie would be about pregnancy. Cue trailer man's voice (his name was Don LaFontaine if you're interested): 'In a world where men get pregnant, one man …

on a journey into the unknown ... must fight chronic nausea and debilitating gas to bring a child into this world.' Starring Matt Damon as the dad-to-be and Russell Crowe as his foetus. *Saving Ryan's Privates* would sweep the Oscars. Yes, I realise that *Saving Ryan's Privates* is already a spoof movie about soldiers saving their comrade's penis and *Shaving Ryan's Privates* is an already-existing porno. And, yes, my search history is a shambles.

I guess I shouldn't be that surprised that this pregnancy has taken such a weird turn. There's nothing so sci-fi in life as reproducing. How do we all go around pretending there's nothing totally crazy about it? As comedian Simon Amstell says of trying to have a conversation with his mother: 'I came out of your vagina, let's not pretend that's a normal thing to have happened.'

It's interesting, given every one of us grew inside a human and many of us will go on to grow our own, that a recurring feature of horror and science fiction is things growing inside us. Watching something wriggling beneath the skin is the stuff of both nightmares – see *Alien* and *Rosemary's Baby* – and cosy ads for home insurance. Other symptoms are less visceral but equally unnerving – the vivid dreams and nightmares in pregnancy are like a foreshadowing of the kind of powerful anxiety that will ultimately stalk us once the bloody thing is out. The new flavour of our subconscious in these months also speaks to the feeling of possession. Not to mention, if you're me, the newfound passion for blood. In *Dracula*, there is repeated reference to illness and the 'stricken land'. Lucy's vitality is drained and drained, and she displays many of the symptoms of pregnancy as Dracula, mostly unseen, feasts on her. I need a Lucy.

I look at my juicy babies and think about Goya's *Saturn Devouring His Son* – from the look on his face it looks to be a joyless meal.

In *Hungry Words*, in her reading of *Dracula* as a Famine text, Sarah Goss quotes the anonymous nineteenth-century Famine poem 'Thanatos':

> A mother's heart was marble-clad, her eye was fierce and
> wild –
> A hungry Demon lurked therein, while gazing on her child.
> The mother-love was warm and true; the Want was long
> withstood –
> Strength failed at last; she gorged the flesh – the offspring
> of her blood.

Course *I* didn't have the excuse of a catastrophic potato blight.

The mother and baby forums on the internet were absolutely no help on the blood craving, but I did find some recognition for my affliction in the 1990 French film *Baby Blood*. It centres around a woman, Yanka, whose womb is taken over by an organism that demands she kill and ingest blood to nourish it. You just love finding common ground with a cannibalism-ridden body horror flick, right? On a warmer note, *Baby Blood* is a great example of the ferocity of a mother's love for her baby. Yanka, despite having no desire to kill, obliges the thing within, even after it tells her its plan to replace humans as the dominant species on Earth.

Tokophobia is a fear of pregnancy and childbirth, and has to be one of the most logical phobias going. It's sensible to be afraid of being inhabited by an unknown quantity, especially one so powerful as to hold sway over your emotions, appetites and dreams. Also some women turn the toilet seat blue while pregnant – what the fuck is that all about? I've seen the blue seat blamed on many things including pregnancy supplements and hormones. Ah, hormones, a great catch all for 'woman stuff'. The various catch-22s of pregnancy mock us. We're desperately uncomfortable but can't take decent painkillers. We're hungry but nauseous. We're occasionally petrified of what's coming but hormonal changes disturb the mechanisms we have for regulating fear and anxiety. Brilliant. Just brilliant.

Other movies of the horror genre mine the paranoid terror of pregnancy and parenthood. *Hungry Hearts* charts a mother's increasingly destructive obsession with what her baby is consuming, until the baby is undernourished and in grave danger. It's a deeply unnerving take on the hyper-cautious parenting so rampant right now and captures the sense of 'damned if you do damned if you don't' that accompanies parenthood.

For me, the blood craving is just the latest catch-22. Blood, blood everywhere but not a drop to drink. I ate black pudding and barely cooked steak and I drank an iron supplement that the pharmacist warned me to mix with orange juice to mask the flavour of iron. I drank it straight, in double doses, and the metallic taste did assuage the blood craving somewhat. It also nixed my iron deficiency, thank god, before I could put any relationships under undue strain by demanding the blood of my friends. I did make other demands of them, however. You see the blood hunger stayed with me beyond the pregnancy. It wasn't fuelled by a baby-in-waiting anymore but instead a rabid curiosity. A rabid curiosity that was stoked by a hilariously innocent source and shows just where a morbid mind can bring you.

I kept thinking of a half-remembered scene from a book of my childhood, *Under the Hawthorn Tree* by Marita Conlon-McKenna. It involved blood-letting at some point, I was sure of it. I bought a copy and devoured it in an evening – fair fecks to Conlon-McKenna, it's as brilliant as ever. The book is about three children trying to find their family in the desperate days of the 1840s when Ireland was starving and wretched. The scene occurs towards the end of the story. The children find a cow and the young boy decides to bleed her. He is careful to find a small vein so that the cow doesn't bleed to death.

> Eily passed him the blade … He deepened the cut and
> a droplet or two of blood appeared. The cow lowed and
> rolled her frightened eyes … Michael was squeezing at
> the opening with his fingers. The blood began to trickle
> and then to flow freely and spatter on the ground …
> The blood seemed to pump quicker and quicker.

The children make themselves a crude blood pudding over a fire, restoring their depleted bodies enough to make it to their relatives. Back when I was pregnant and the bloodlust was at its peak, I'd been snobby about the blood of animals. But what did I think? That I was born better? Time to stoop, I decided. If only to rid myself of the fiendish fervour.

I asked after pig's blood from a few butchers. One promised to have it in a few days for me. Reader, I rang every day for five days. I was overzealous, shall we say. The butcher eventually broke the news that he wouldn't be able to get me any blood at that time. I was beside myself. I'd wasted five days waiting. I took my ghoulish custom to another butcher who was amused but a lot more helpful. He would have three litres of blood for me that very afternoon. A snag. Due to a close contact having Covid, I was in self-isolation at this time and unable to leave my house. At this point, I'd been in isolation for eight days. This may or may not have something to do with the events that followed.

I have a WhatsApp group that goes by the emoji of a tomato. It's a historical reference to what I now can't remember. Both of these friends live close to the butcher in question. There was nothing for it – I texted:

Me: Hello Dublin 8 pals! Just wondering if either of you wud be free to do me a wee favour this afternoon. No stress if not.

EML: I can! As long as I don't have to lick or touch anyone.

EOMD: I am in work til 7 but I can, I will.

Me: Ye're the best.

Me: The item is unorthodox.

EML: Ooh.

Me: 3 litres of pig's blood.

EML: Omg are you making pudding? Or doing a Carrie on someone.

EOMD: Was just about to type that. That is so gross but … carry on.

Me: Yes I am, it is vaguely work-related.

EML: Do you have it ordered or do I need to march in and say 'THREE PINTS OF PIG BLOOD PLEASE'.

Me: You can say 'my weird friend was on to u bout
the blood!'

EML: Lol okay. I love a task.

I have such supportive friends.

'They're ENABLERS,' Seb later raged. He didn't love it
when the three litres of blood, transported in a large milk
bottle, arrived at the door. My four-year-old insisted he
bring it to the kitchen. He's in the helpful phase. The thing
was heavy and about the same size as him. It was tense. He
barely had a grip on it and it was dropping further to the
floor with every shaky step he took. He didn't drop it, and
into the fridge it went as I prepared the ingredients for
the blood pudding I was going to make. I had to wait till
a good moment when the kids were out as they are glued
to me at all times, especially when I'm doing something
that will intrigue them. And given that they're my kids I
presumed this would intrigue them.

I tried to draw out the experience of the blood, to
extract as much from each element – the smell, the texture,
the flavour – as I could. I unscrewed the lid and inhaled
deeply. This was the first sign that there might be a problem.
It didn't smell like anything much. So disappointing. The
liquid iron supplement I took when pregnant had more of
a reek. I pressed on. The first step was to salt it and then pass
it through a sieve. For the moment of pouring, I got low to

the bowl to witness the gush. To commune with it (I had gone full Joseph Beuys at this point). I expected it to be an incredibly thick and lush syrup, lovely meat syrup, but it looked to be only a fraction thicker than water, if even. I couldn't believe it. I know you're wondering and yes I did have a taste, a little one, but it just confirmed that whatever that lusty appetite had been for, this wasn't it. Even the black pudding it yielded was a bit meh.

Disappointed with the flaccid end to my adventures in blood I decided to throw everything at it and do the only remaining thing I could think of. I'm very aware that this bit will be divisive because this was the moment when I truly jumped the shark. You may remember that part of the fantasy had been crouching under a pristine sheet of blood …

Now. I know what you're thinking and, friend, you would be right.

I did indeed kneel in my bath, hold the container aloft and pour the remaining two litres of blood over my body.

And?

Nothing. Absolutely nothing. As Marie Kondo would say, 'it did not spark joy'. Though it does offer final proof, should we have needed it, that you can take the art student out of art school but you cannot take art school out of the art student.

If I'd still been possessed by the foetus this could've gone some way towards excusing this behaviour. 'What about the isolation!' I protest. 'Eight days! It's been very trying.' Fine, fine, I'll accept your judgment. But do not let it be said that I am anything less than completely and utterly determined and willing to let my creep flag fly for the sake of experimentation.

I should have called this essay 'What the actual fuck, Sophie?', shouldn't I? or 'I got *Carried* away'.

DRUNK GIRL

When you're an alcoholic, it's no mystery. It's a piece of knowledge lodged in your psyche since always. It's not a concept that you want to consider, so you push it aside. Push it down. Put something heavy on top of it, drown it with rationalisations or, better, booze. Never look at the thing. Never look at that ravenous thing, never *know* it. Never know the truest thing you know about yourself.

From the first drink, I knew. This was divine. This would be disastrous. This glass, this bottle, this drink would never be enough. I have drained every glass. I've drained every party. I've drained people who minded me while hiding their disgust at me. I've drained myself most of all. Consuming and being subsumed: it's an exhausting occupation. Enough will always be a difficult concept for me.

What I've learned in sobriety is that drinkers are mostly all the same, so I'll try not to bore you. While the facts of different drinkers' lives differ and our habits diverge, the drive behind the thankless task of slow death by consumption is, by and large, the same – a dark melody in the same key.

What I was looking for at all times was an escape hatch, a way out of the present moment, to tunnel out of my totally unremarkable and pathetic self. To break the cycle of being a terminal disappointment: a disappointment as a daughter, a mother, a woman, failing at that implied contract of womanhood – of being nice and attractive and contained.

I believed I was never enough and, in turn, nothing I heaped into this banal void of a person was ever enough. Somehow I managed to be both too much and not enough. A feat of neuroses! And for such a long time this endless swallowing worked.

At the start, my drinking obeyed the tacit agreement that it would accommodate my life, it wouldn't spill out and muddy my outward appearance, it would just gouge at me little by little, quietly out of sight. By the end, though, it ran in my veins along with my blood and had begun to seep through my carefully maintained veneer of normality – a veneer that was a full-time job to maintain.

In the early years, logistics kept me somewhat out of reach of this irresistible substance. It was mainly just hard to get a hold of as a teenager. When I did, it rarely ended well.

When I drank in my teens I nearly always blacked out for stretches of the night. The black-outs strike me as terrifying now. I was forever stumbling beside an edge, weaving closer and closer to calamity, only for dumb luck to save me each time. The dumb luck could only stretch so far. While it saved me from grave physical injury, it left me with a deeper bruise: shame at the half-remembered things I did and the things that happened in my waking sleep.

With some practice, I realised I could extract the events of the blank hours and discard them. They didn't happen in any real way, I convinced myself. From this safe distance I can only gather together glimpses of this thankfully fairly tame teenage rampage. I see myself as I always do: gross, swaying and miserable, but unable to articulate why.

There were good times too, of course: laughing and teenage romantic intrigue, hours talking to my friends about what, I can't even fathom. I was so unformed – we all were. God I hated my teens. I was obsessed with the useless things that trouble most teenagers. I had a gnawing longing to be different to the useless thing I was. Being an ugly girl felt like one of the most useless things you could be. And, like most teenage girls, I thought I was ugly. There I was, without purpose, my body stubbornly refusing to be of value, my face an affront. I genuinely felt apologetic for being ugly, sensing I wasn't fulfilling my side of the deal.

Numbness was my great pursuit. I loved to drink, and then I loved to smoke hash, and then in college I loved to swallow pills and magic mushrooms. The idea that I crammed things down in an uneasy fashion has nagged at me since I first began to hide my insatiable ways. I ate in secret as a child; it was so much more relaxing to hide away and worship that little compulsion on my own without judgment or putting on some pesky pretence that food was the same for me as it was for everyone else. Much later, I would find the exact same thing with alcohol. I suppose you'd call it a red flag. But I didn't. I was perpetrating such a level of self-deception that I could see nothing strange about my life. Even though by the end I hardly drank with other people at all – the work of hiding my need made it too much of a headache to do in the presence of other people.

In college, I was still an embarrassment. I floundered. I picked up personas and drugs and drinks and friends and strange men and sometimes women and was perpetually uneasy. I existed unsteadily, always on the cusp of toppling all the way over.

I have a montage of shame from that time. It's a collection of senseless exploits – a one-night stand with a man who dresses as a cowboy, me singing 'Always Look On the Bright Side of Life' on a damp 3am street and being head-butted by a random man. Being pushed by a stranger into a wall in Paris. Eating cereal in bed with a boy I liked as he told me he didn't want me. Being kissed by the same boy some years later and choosing instead to reject him and 'win', rather than be happy and kiss him back. I was scared of sincerity; I think it was a symptom of growing up in the jaded nineties. Heaven for-fucking-bid someone should have a feeling and express it.

I was an unbearable pastiche of nineties apathy. I blame my choice in books and TV. I watched the MTV animation *Daria*, which followed a misanthropic high-school student and her best friend trapped in nondescript American suburbia. Daria railed against the mindless optimism of her peers and I immediately understood that accessorising with a jaded sardonic cynicism was much safer than dabbling in vulnerability of any kind. As a teen, when sincere people were sincere in my presence, I filed them under 'uncool', that most damning of teenage insults. Instead, I searched out other ennui-touting yet hilariously middle-class youths like myself. Their affected cool no doubt covered up the same fear of being found out that mine did. I also think an ill-advised early reading of Bret Easton Ellis's *Less Than Zero* did me no favours. I didn't read it in its intended context of critiquing a certain type of rich, stupid narcissism. I just thought this hedonistic, contemporary Holden Caulfield was fascinating and to be emulated. Oh dear.

Towards the end of college, I loved magic mushrooms. If you're looking for an escape hatch there's no finer substance. What better escape than sliding right out of reality altogether? I still marvel at the beauty the human brain is capable of conjuring when you ply it with just the right thing. However, I can never revisit those melting, morphing splendid nights without acknowledging that in direct proportion to the beauty, the brain can savage us too. I learned that later, but the early days with drugs were just magic. I distinctly remember thinking: 'If life can be like this then I'm in', as if at twenty I'd still been undecided.

But the bawling appetite is an exhausting thing to tame.

So how low did I go?

I plummeted, but largely I plummeted in plain sight. You can do that with alcoholism, especially here where I'm from. You can go really low, especially if you're willing to be a joke.

There's something very particularly abhorrent about a drunk girl. A sickly desperation rolls off her like a stench. She teeters and topples, knees scuffed. She deserves nothing. No justice if she is victimised by an opportunistic predator. Opportunistic – it's a word that practically commends this tenacious, moment-seizing, go-getting rapist. A drunk girl is a site for scorn and blame and pity. She is an object of hate. An object. No one is more convinced of this than the object itself.

The summer I was thirty-two, I was in trouble. On the face of it I was coping extremely well. My dad had died in May. I had started a new job the same month. My second child was five months old. While my life was hectic and my every moment filled to bursting with babies and work and deadlines, my mind lapsed into a period of stasis. I was mentally immobilised. It was a colossal effort to hold things together, myself included. I was drinking more and more heavily, but still showing up for the things I had to show up for.

In late summer, I went to a festival and felt palpable relief at what I saw as an opportunity to let go. I had some work commitments over the course of the weekend, but I was free from the work of living for a few days in the kind of environment that had always provided the perfect cover for my obsession. I had always found, paradoxically, that my drinking would calm down in those circumstances. I could slow down. An easiness that was strangely absent from my normal-life drinking would emerge.

It makes a skewed sense if you are me, or at least someone like me. When I would drink with other people in restaurants or at parties, it took a concerted effort to appear normal in my consumption. Social drinking required a constant self-management that was so tiresome, I preferred to devote myself in private by the end. So perhaps you can understand how much of a relief it was to feel like I was for once on the same level as the rest of the world, if only for a few days. To not have to watch myself or watch them watching me.

The first night I drank so much that I lost my friend and was once more stumbling along an unseen edge. I had left my phone with my friend and wandered into a night that heaved with bodies. I may as well have walked off a cliff. It would take divine intervention to bring us back together in that vast crowd, and that was if I had been sober. In my tipsy state, I didn't stand a chance. But then I saw something that looked like good news. A familiar face. Not that familiar, more a friend of friends who I'd gone to college with. He was a quiet man I'd met here and there over the years.

'I've fucking lost everyone,' I laughed when he came towards me on the edge of a field, mayhem around us, summer stars overhead.

I don't seem to remember him answering, just smiling. I don't think any nefarious plan swelled behind that smile. We all know that's not always how it happens.

'I can't even find our campsite and they've got my phone,' I flailed and shrugged and grinned because in truth I wasn't all that concerned. I was enjoying the freedom of fucking up in relative safety, shrugging off the pressing angst of being a mother and a daughter and a wife for a few sweet hours. 'Can I call it from yours?'

'Sure …' we walked together and I tried my number a few times, mainly to assuage any worry on the part of my pal.

'Can I stay with you guys?'

'Sure ...'

We walked on to where he was camped. I was almost bored in this scenario – the night winding down to a banal chat in some folding lawn chairs. Around us people were still pursuing possibilities but for us it was just some chit-chat and then, seeing the night had dwindled, I tried my phone one last time and then crawled into the tent to sleep.

At some point in the next few hours, this man – perhaps buoyed by an inherited sense of entitlement so total and profound that it will forever confound me – began to use my unconscious body.

When I woke up I froze. For a confused moment I thought the presence behind me was my husband but as the thoughts fell into order and the last hours of the previous night came back I realised what was going on.

I felt a gut-punch of disgust. With myself.

This was clearly my fault, in what way exactly, I would work out later. For now it was most important that I extract myself without making a fuss and risk a tedious scenario becoming potentially volatile.

In terms of being touched without my consent, this incident factors pretty low in the litany of what I have come to call Violation Lite, but the aftermath ended up being quite revelatory.

Back in the moment of this grasping, pushy, sicken-ing embrace I pretended to still be asleep. I debated my choices and concluded that any kind of confrontation was pointless; acknowledging what was happening would force me to confront whatever my part in it was and I was too ashamed. I sat bolt upright and in one swift movement crawled out into the dawn. My body fizzed and flexed for a fight I was sure I wouldn't need to have but still you can never be certain. That had been one of my mistakes the night before after all, certain in my safety with a familiar face.

I grabbed my shoes in the damp morning grass. I stormed across the field, eyes straight ahead before I reached an empty back road and then broke into a run. The effort – my lungs scalded, the pounding of my shoes on gravel – was all I could do to drown out the refrain of self-loathing that had started up. When I'd put about a mile between myself and that stifling, shameful moment, I slowed and began a pitiless interrogation of myself.

'You were drunk.'

I was.

'You were alone.'

I was.

'You were alone because you were drunk.'

I was.

'You went with him.'

I did.

'You got into the tent first.'

I did.

'You did something to make him think that touching you was ok.'

Did I?

'You went with him.'

I did. That's enough I guess.

'What were you wearing?'

A navy dress. Sandals.

'Well.'

It's not even low-cut.

'It's a dress, I can see your legs. And you were drunk. You were drunk. You were drunk.'

I was drunk.

A part of me screamed, 'Would you ask your friend these questions? Would you allow another woman to blame herself for this? For having the gall to sleep in the presence of a man? Are we blaming women for this now?'

But I didn't listen to that part of me. Even writing this after the fact, I have to remind myself it's not my fault. This is the message we've ingested. This is what's been peddled to us. I can picture the boardroom pitch now:

Marketing Exec: Get this! We'll use them and hurt them and then – here's the genius bit – they blame themselves!

As I said, I filed this incident under Violation Lite. I've been trained to. Most women, I tell myself, have experienced some riff on this kind of scenario at points in their lives and of course many have experienced far worse. When I was younger, my instinct was to downplay it. After some scathing victim-blaming of myself, I would berate myself for making a big deal out of something that everyone has to put up with one way or another and then move on. I'd bury the feeling until it no longer caused me to cringe at my disgusting and shameful ways. *My* disgusting and shameful ways. Not the ways of the men. Not the man who grabbed my barely-there breasts when I was thirteen and had the temerity to be simply walking through a crowd at a concert. Or the man who touched my lips and stroked my face while I sat on the train in my school uniform. Or the various men I've encountered around the place wanking as I've been going about my day.

Sidenote: I swear this being wanked-at is a thing. It's happened to me at least three times. What goes through their minds? What do they think we'll say? 'I'm so touched, I had no idea you felt that way'?

Here is another story.

One I've talked myself into and out of relating endlessly – debating if it is even worthy of discussion. But anyway … I've always had a very strong conviction that I am a fundamentally bad person for reasons undefined. Recently, I was reading about the serial killer Denis Rader, also known as BTK. An evil individual. Truly. A murderer who tortured and degraded and visited suffering of a magnitude impossible to grasp on his victims and their loved ones. I was disgusted and horrified at what I read and then I had the thought, *Sure I'm no better than BTK*. It's totally illogical and objectively not true, but this is the level of wrongness I often feel. I say 'often' but really I mean whenever I give it even a second's thought because the feeling is always there. I asked my mother:

> Me: Do you ever feel like a really bad person? Like irredeemably wrong, bad to your core?
>
> My mother: No.

Don't rush to reassure me or anything.

Anyway, this unshakable sense of wrongness has been there since I was a small child. It had nothing to do with my family who were, and are, incredibly loving. It just seemed to take hold one day. And even though I frequently dismiss this event and tell myself I'm making a big deal out of nothing, I think about this incident a lot and I remember feeling very altered by it.

We had just moved house. I am four. They are ten or eleven. They do things to me and make me do things to them. When we are discovered, there is trouble. The knowledge that this Wrong Thing is my fault, is *still* my fault, is as real and solid to me as the table I sit at right now. The knowledge has been knit into the tissue and muscle and bones of me. I did that Wrong Thing. I am now a mother of boys. I know four-year-olds and I know ten- and eleven-year-olds. I think now, on an academic level, that I am not entirely to blame for the Wrong Thing. But I feel and know on an *atomic* level that I am. The shame is more powerful than the logic. It cannot be reasoned with. Interrogating the memories, the damning evidence I come up with to support my revolting culpability is a silk dressing gown. It is white with a piped trim and I was baiting these boys with my dressing gown and my blameless four-year-old body. I know four-year-olds. I know my best friend's beautiful four-year-old daughter. She loves dressing up. She would flounce and dance and twirl around in a silk dressing gown. *And she wouldn't fucking mean anything by it, Sophie*, I scream at myself. Still, the whisper of doubt is insistent.

I was a four-year-old who *was* asking for it.

I think the adults did their best with the Wrong Thing. It's hard to haul something like that right out into the open. To tease it apart and set it right, especially since setting it right could have 'ramifications' for the boys involved. It's easier to boil it down to something more manageable and recognisable, like kids exploring or boys being boys. But what are the ramifications of letting it slide? Did those boys grow up to help themselves to other girls? Sleeping girls? Drunk girls?

I tried to let it slide but it lingers in the bloodstream. Rationalising really will only get you so far.

Everyone experiences stuff like that, the hectoring voice says. *It's just boys being boys*. The perceived inaction by the adults seemed to support this.

Get over it, four-year-old girl.

When I was twenty, I saw one of the boys in a shop. It was destabilising. I'd thought about the Wrong Thing several times a year, but I'd never been able to put something as logical and definitive as words to it. The memories were less defined than that. Shame would steal through my body and the feelings of that day – the sick certainty that I was a disgusting, dirty and undeserving little person – would course through me once more.

Although sixteen years had passed, the day I saw him my shame surfaced and latched to him as though drawn out by a powerful magnet. A logical part of me thought,

You can't be sure that it's him. It's been years and anyway that was just kids being kids and never mind that there were two of them and one of you and never mind that you were four and they were ten or eleven. But the reaction in my limbs was unmistakable; I shook and thrummed with the invasion as though it was happening all over again. The Wrong Thing had happened and just because it was murky and nuanced and commonplace and just because there was a silk goddamn robe didn't mean that it hadn't played some part in my life and denying The Wrong Thing or mini-mising it would not change that.

Also perhaps the ubiquity of these wrong things, rather than allowing them to be glossed over, should be all the more reason to do something about them.

So back to the tent in the field, and the latest in the line of common, irrelevant Wrong Things.

I tentatively tell my friend, skimming the surface of the incident. I think it was a litmus test, asking her to resolve my guilt and apportion the blame. Her initial response betrays a glimpse of the same deeply ingrained misogyny all women struggle with. We've ingested the message over and over. It's in the air we breath. It's a Kool-Aid we swallow that slyly makes us collude with the system that has never protected us or valued us or believed us.

She swiftly self-corrects, as many of us have to when grappling with these stories. She understands. I understand. I'll absorb this thing because to do anything otherwise could have 'consequences' for this man. And me. And I'll absorb this thing because I was drunk and in being a drunk girl I have forfeited my right to not be treated like an object. I have devalued myself and made myself the perfect scapegoat for this murky, tricky, hard-to-quite-pin-down and all too fucking common situation.

But do you think it's wrong to touch an unconscious person? If confronted with a sleeping person, would your instinct be to seek some grim gratification? It does seem a bit off, doesn't it? But anyway, I'll absorb it. Obviously. It's murky. It's tricky. It's nuanced. I was a drunk girl and therefore not the right kind of girl for this to matter. It wasn't that bad, I repeat to myself. And it wasn't, of course, it wasn't. But what does it take for these things to matter?

'When he put his hand on my thigh I felt myself leaving this casket. Is it really rape if I never said no. Is it really abuse if I don't have the scars to prove it' rages the spoken word poet Jenifer Williams.

Why must women endure the very worst to prove a truth that's visible every single time we excuse the awful boys? That or downplay their cruelty and entitlement.

I don't make a fuss. My husband arrives and I don't tell him. Funny to think that those who love us have no knowledge of what our bodies contain, a shame soup of gropes and yanks and pushes and punches and thrusts, just kept from bleeding into our lives. Kept at bay by our skin, a membrane so easily torn is all that keeps these Wrong

Things from tainting everything. And of course it can't hold, it won't.

There are two bawling reasons as to why I don't tell him. One: that he won't believe that it's not my fault; two: that he will, and all that that will entail.

Usually men are not so well-versed in the art of swallowing shame and anger. They tend to turn it outward rather than inward – most of the time that's more a woman's game – and I cannot bear the mess of that.

The next day it is a little easier to push the new Wrong Thing down; it rears up occasionally and I push it back. I drink steadily, which helps subdue it. I have to go and give a reading in a tent full of smiling, relaxed people. I am pacing in front of the crowd and acting out parts of the essay I am reading when I see him come in. Just like when I was twenty and I felt the boy's proximity before my eyes even found him, here now the same magnetic force draws my ignominy out, tentacle-like.

A shame-fug radiates from me. Our shame is how they leverage us and make us shoulder the blame for their actions. In our shame, they spy us doubting ourselves and they gouge at this sliver of doubt when they describe the myriad ways we invited this thing until the culpability is ours and ours alone. This is how they game our shame. I just wish we weren't a sport.

Without breaking from the reading, I am suddenly taming an onslaught of panicked thoughts. *What's he doing here? Is he here to intimidate me? Or does he think nothing of what happened? That it's no big deal that he shows up here right now? Or he's here to apologise? Or to tell my husband that I was a drunk, disgusting girl who slept in his presence and therefore deserved nothing better than to be molested?*

I have thought and thought and thought about why he showed up and the best I can come up with is that somehow in his mind, using me while I slept was no biggie.

And he thinks that because we let him think that. Don't we?

SELF-SOOTHING

I went to a festival two weeks after my dad died, and blurted into the middle of a pleasant, ordinary conversation, 'My dad died the week before last.' It was simply a fact that couldn't be helped. The week will come in all our lives when it's a week and a half after a cataclysmic loss – the two things so wildly at odds, one an unbelievable aberration, the other a mundane metric of time. However, my flat affect was, I see now, odd. Not making a big deal of it. I can see now that acting outwardly throwaway about the death of a loved one was fucking weird. I thought downplaying it was coping.

At what point does coping become corrosive? Up till then, you'd never have caught me displaying any signs of anguish. It is a very dubious badge of honour. Where did this need to appear to be unfeeling come from? This may seem outlandish but I genuinely blame the nineties. It was a very disturbing time to grow up. Not as disturbing as now, of course – this pastel dystopia where people glue extra bits of hair and plastic to their bodies is wildly weirder. But still, the nineties were a time.

In my teens, we wore our glib apathy as an accessory, like our studded dog collars and parachute pants. It was trying for me because I was actually an innate emoter and a massive cry-baby, especially in my early teens, but I gradually got the memo: feelings are weak. Remember the teen landscape is littered with unholy bitches just waiting to tear you down. I got older and it became anathema to be visibly vulnerable. In my late teens, a close friend tried to take their own life, and it seemed preferable to pretend to be bored by this horrific episode rather than troubled. Anything rather than express a feeling.

Feelings were a terrible encumbrance back then; it was deeply uncool to have any at all. You wouldn't have been caught dead *daring bravely* in that decade of studied indifference. I think *A Heartbreaking Work of Staggering Genius* was the beginning and end of my emotional education as a teenager. I envied Eggers' sly cool when it came to his personal tragedy – both his parents died within a month of each other and he had to raise his eight-year-old brother. I vividly remember his audition for MTV's *Real World* in the book, when he describes with self-referential irony how, should he be selected, he can make his trauma 'play' any way.

'I can do it funny, or maudlin, or just straight, uninflected – anything. You tell me. I can do it sad, or inspirational, or angry,' he tells the TV executive.

This is where I got the idea that it's not cool to be sad or affected deeply by the things that happen to you. Be callous or calculating, just don't be wholehearted, it's too risky.

And I think this contributed, at least in part, to our generational instinct to suppress unpleasant feelings at all costs, rather than allow them to be exorcised in tears or rage. Hence our jealousy a decade later when the next cohort – who we've mockingly dubbed the Snowflakes – wisely opted not to perpetuate this impotent and damaging affected stoicism.

Maybe this lack of outlet is why my monstrous hands have always soothed me. I say 'monstrous' because, while they've soothed me, they have also been the undoing of me. They were the purveyors of narcotic solutions to difficult feelings: drugs and wine – putting various things in my mouth. These are the things that worked with varying success for years, until they didn't.

A far better success story than drugs, on the other hand, is simply stoppering the mouth altogether. Just as I don't remember a time before words, I don't remember a time before my thumb. Mostly, science agrees that thumbsucking starts in utero and about 10 per cent of people persist with it into adulthood. I think of it more as the thumb persisting. It's an involuntary action on my part. I've usually only realised I'm doing it because of the reaction of those around me. Their features reshuffle to surprised amusement or intense fascination and I realise it's happening. I'm being a thirty-something 'serious lady' sucking her thumb at a meeting or the cinema or a restaurant. This has rarely tipped into problematic territory, thankfully. Except for the people who think the thumb-sucking is my coy hint at some invisible-to-the-naked-eye erotic undertones. Seeing as I have this unique opportunity to clarify: it's not. I always thought of it as a nice bit of relaxing. It's hard to compare the sensation to anything more universal. It's not like eating when you're really hungry, nor like a narcotic rush. It's not a feeling of *adding* to the equation but rather a setting of something to rights. It's close to the feeling I used to get from the first much-anticipated glass of wine when I was an active alcoholic.

Sidenote: That's the lingo, pals. To differentiate my dormant (never extinct, never truly vanquished) alcoholism from my hale-and-hearty, climb-a-mountain, jump-in-a-lake *active* alcoholism.

Think of the feeling of comfort returning. The gasping relief of stopping after running full tilt. Slipping my thumb into where it belongs, gently clamped between tongue and palette, is my resetting to neutral. If I'm really settling in, the fingers of my right hand will find some hair and begin a little repetitive ritual of twisting, crunching and pressing. If I'm really getting into it, the fingers of the left hand get involved. I keep the nail of my fourth finger slightly long so that I can run a looped piece of hair under it, over and over.

Writing this feels funny: it feels as intimate as telling you about my masturbatory preferences. The mouth is an intrinsically intimate space; it's a passage that is neither internal nor external. The pink soft tissue is outrageously sensual when you think of it. It's an absence and an undulating organ at the same time, just like the vagina. Maybe it's me who's being facetious announcing there's no eroticism to be found in the soothing sucking.

And of course masturbation is one of the great soothers in this life too, even among children. I often imagine that the original soother was invented by some hysterical devout parent to keep the kids from getting too hands-on with themselves. Though digging around the internet, I learn that the OG soothers were often rags dipped in brandy, or stuffed with poppy seeds, which seems to bring us full circle to the more socially accepted narcotic self-soothing of contemporary times.

So there I am hunched, sucking, sucking, sucking and tugging and twisting my hair.

After more than a decade of dispatching feelings both good and bad with every predictable substance available, I feel I've actually come to a point where I would have something to offer students of a coping class.

I've come to realise that it's not my duty to not disturb other people with my pain – it is my duty to metabolise these feelings, face them, handle them even though grief is painful to touch. It is actually more selfish to smother it and tamp it down. What's braver and ultimately safer is to own up to it. To look right at it and name it: I am desperately sad. I'm so sad that I have turned on myself because it simply feels so unacceptable to turn these feelings outward. I was wrongly commending myself for never breaking down, for never crying, for holding myself in check. Pain will not be stamped down and neutralised, for having an inburst instead of an outburst. If you don't address it and connect with it and accept it, it will become toxic and infect the people you love. Now I highly recommend having an outburst. Fucking scream if it hurts. Not screaming could prove fatal.

My other method of self-soothing is less adorable than my babyish thumb-sucking. I think we sometimes see self-harming as a self-indulgent sort of exhibitionism. It calls to mind teenage eye-rolling and emo angst. I felt that too, and still do to some extent. It is mortally embarrassing to admit to it here but having crawled inside the strangely comforting realm of inflicting this pain on myself, I can report it is a compulsion and as my psychiatrist said 'more a symptom of a problem rather than necessarily a problem in and of itself'.

I can't exactly remember when it started, but I do remember that when I had my babies was when I finally had to consciously acknowledge it, because now I was hurting a shared thing. My body was their home and so hurting it required new stealth on my part. Their existence forced me to confront this thing I needed to do from time to time. Before, I could rake my nails across my scalp, pinch and scratch my flesh, bite my hands and hit my head on the wall when the shriek inside overwhelmed. It was a desperate but satisfying release.

I was capable of unleashing this passive abuse and move on with barely a moment's pause. I never wondered at it because I was fundamentally embarrassed by it. The most acknowledgment of it I would allow would be a sneering thought: *You're so pathetic*, or *This is the most privileged, first-world bullshit of all time, get a real problem*, and then I'd move on with my day.

After the babies were born and began to roam my soft, useless morass of a body, it brought a new shame around my self-harming. Because certainly in the first years of their lives – while they may have left the cavity of my womb, they didn't go far – it began to feel like I was inflicting a communal punishment. Their juicy new bodies were a relative of my own; they matched me; their skin had the same texture and hue of my skin. And hurting myself began to feel like hurting them.

As babies, we are incredibly possessive of and fascinated by our mothers' bodies. We perch on their hips and burrow into their comforting warmth. It's impossible to imagine such proximity in maturity. We'll never know another closeness like it. Cuddling is more fleeting, sex often strangely solitary despite the connection, but being held as a baby is a complete merging. For months or even years, our experience is buffered by the body of our mother. She is the ship on which we sail. A sanctuary. A home.

When my body became home to my babies, my mistreatment of it began to shame me more and more. Instead of revelling in our strange and fundamental connection that seemed to defy description, I was scared of it. I was frightened of what they saw in me when I loomed over their field of vision. You cannot live in such certainty of your own wrongness and not be constantly terrified that others will detect it too.

In the most literal sense, I was spoiling their home, polluting the food supply. Consuming myself with an appetite that couldn't be sated with either booze or food. It was as though I'd entered a phase of hunger that was beyond placating with mere *things*, where instead physical pain was providing me with gratification.

And, more worrying than anything, presumably I was teaching them to torture themselves too one day. As Father Richard Rohr wrote, 'If we do not transform our pain, we will most assuredly transmit it – usually to those closest to us'.

Having tried every easy way in which to dispatch pain – yes, self-harm, be it through food, drink, drugs and mauling your own flesh, is comparatively easy compared with acceptance – I have finally come to something of a solution. Sit with it. Submerge yourself into the frightening unknown of it. You won't get lost, which I think is our prevailing fear.

After I had my first baby, I was manic. I swung between elation and anxiety, terrified to trust myself with my tiny precious son. I begged to stay in hospital, trying to avoid the formless dread I was convinced lay beyond those walls. 'Surely everyone begs to stay?' I argued after the midwife had shook her head kindly. She was mystified at my refusal to leave. 'But you can bring your baby home today,' she said.

She didn't get that to me in this new world, there was nothing more sinister than 'home'. I wanted my son and I to be confined and monitored forever now. I wanted to inoculate us against every potential danger that lay ahead. I wanted to be placed under observation forever, or at least until my son was raised and had survived my mothering unscathed. I was wild with these new fears. Life now seemed to contain despair beyond anything I'd previously conceived of. I oscillated between clinging to the new boy and ignoring him in his plastic crib. I was scared of him and I'd also fallen for him. Hard. Like psycho hard. *Save him from me*, I wanted to shout at the midwife. She calmly suggested I go and have a cry in the shower.

'Go in there and let it all out.' She was scarily intuitive.

'I can't,' I said.

'Why not?'

'Because I'll start and it'll never stop.'

I got in the shower and roared. The situation felt desperate. Blood leaked onto the tiles. It was a horror show. In the corner of the shower, there was a stool presumably haunted with the anguish of all the other women who had stood here broken by the new love that was so unexpectedly harsh – so tinged with pain and awe and foreboding. Jesus Christ how did Kate Middleton get a blow-dry and put on a dress after this thing?

I cried, and after a while it actually did subside. I got dressed, feeling like I hadn't touched the bottom of that despair, but it had been appeased for another few days or weeks.

In my son's first year, the events of my life yanked at me mercilessly. I was caring for both my new baby and my father, who was dropping out of sight at a rate of knots. One day, confused, he grabbed my hand and bit it, and I felt sorry for myself. This self that had become progressively cowed and battered by its situation; it struck me how wrong things were going for this body. A baby had been sliced out of it; I laid into it for being soft and useless. I drove it forward with a manic dedication to appearing 'fine', like nothing at all was going on. I catalogued its food and soothed it with booze instead of compassion. Then I clawed it and hit it and now it was bitten by a man who I could barely believe was my father, so ravaged was he by his illness.

I remember leaving him that night and feeling close to screaming, but even as an overwhelming despair seemed poised to break over me, I felt I had no right to this grief. This wasn't happening to *me*, the inner monologue hissed. My beautiful father was losing his mind; my mother was losing her husband – I was just being self-absorbed, it spat. I sat in my car and, instead of crying, I slid my thumb into my mouth and sucked, and when that didn't work, I ground my teeth down into the flimsy skin and hard bone underneath. And that seemed to do the trick. My bites didn't break the skin, but purple marks came up and I cringed that anyone might notice that I self-harm and, worse, don't even do it with much conviction. I am not a cutter – I am a scratcher and a puncher. Cutting seemed too definitive a violence for me; scratching and pinching and hitting seemed conveniently closer to the kinds of touching we might all do in the course of having a body. The boundary of when scratching crosses from appeasing a tickle on the skin to inflicting pain is undefined, especially if you don't look directly at the thing you're doing. Likewise, a fist connecting to a head can be a mere clip or it can be focused and savage and really who's to say at exactly what moment one thing becomes the other? This probably sounds unhinged to anyone who isn't trying to frantically rationalise their self-harming.

'I only self-harm a bit!' When I was a teenager, I worried at my skin with a needle once. My friend, on seeing it, was furious. I think she thought it was pathetic attention-seeking, which at the time I very much agreed with. It was the last time I was careless with the evidence of my little habit.

An early study of self-harming, which appeared in *Anomalies and Curiosities of Medicine* (1896), talked of the so-called 'needle girls': young women who stuck themselves with needles and glass and other objects. The authors George Gould and Walter Pyle classed this self-injury as a form of hysteria – that catch-all malady of women – and those who engaged in it as deceitful and just looking for notice. As recently as the late 1990s, most clinical literature still equated self-harm with severe psychiatric disorders until they realised how bloody common it was.

In the early 2000s, psychologist Janis Whitlock published a study of self-injury. The results were shocking (or comforting if, like me, you're looking for confirmation that hurting yourself isn't the most unstable thing you can do): 20 per cent of women and 14 per cent of men said they had self-injured at least once. Even more revelatory was the fact that the group were young people at Ivy League universities. They were not prisoners of extreme mental illness. They were not compromised severely by social and economic hindrances. They were seemingly high functioning. This provides me with even more slightly incongruous comfort. Sure we're all at it, I tell myself.

But why? The question pummels me. After my second baby is born and my dad dies, my drinking is peaking, and along with it my self-harm. I give in to it because it feels like the safest way for me to rage and grieve without alienating friends and family, but really it still doesn't seem right. Does it? I reluctantly start to analyse it.

I learn that the processing of emotional pain in the brain is closely knit with the processing of physical pain, which makes sense to me. It is always when the rage is bearing down on me that I need to visit the soothing pain on myself. It reroutes the fury, mutating it into something so much more quantifiable and therefore manageable. I am no longer blazing with wild, frightening, rampaging anger; it is replaced by mere hurting. So much more preferable.

As the 'needle girls' article suggests, self-harm is often seen as more of a woman's thing, and while this assumption is wrong, I wonder – in the aftermath of a bout of impressively contained, expertly modulated violence in the privacy of my office – if we were taught how to express our anger as women whether we would still be dragging our fingers across our flesh or sticking them down our throats half as much.

If we were more frank about grief, told grief will be constantly shape-shifting and it won't necessarily be sad but will hurt, that it will possess you and suffocate, maybe I'd have been more ready for it then. Instead, I'm left managing this futile impulse that would be verging on slapstick if it wasn't so pathetic.

You're a joke. I harangue and bully myself endlessly. *You don't matter. You are worthless. None of this pathetic posturing even matters.* That's the terrible trick of mental illness. *You. Don't. Matter.* The stigma of mental illness feels like it's been vanquished sometimes. We talk more openly, we have hashtags and awareness weeks, but the ingrained messages still come and they come from our illness. We whisper them to ourselves in the night. *You. Deserve. This. You. Don't. Matter. You. Don't. Deserve. Help. You. Are. Pathetic. Being mentally ill is bullshit, everyone else can cope – why can't you?*

That I self-harm is one of the most shameful things about me. More than any other story in the book, I wanted to bin this one. It's the grossest thing I do. While there are people whose bodies have failed them, including people I love, and people whose bodies are hurt and stigmatised and murdered by our very society, here I am damaging my perfectly healthy, privileged-as-fuck-one. You think I don't know that's disgusting behaviour? I do.

DRUNK MOTHER

My final year of drinking was profoundly dull. That time in my life wasn't louche and decadent: it was a slow drowning by low-key misery. Looking back now, I realise that after my second baby was born, I began to split in two. I began to hide my behaviours, from anyone who'd care and most especially from myself. I was going through the motions of my life, but only a tiny portion of me was engaged – the rest of me was in a permanent frenzy of calculations:

What time is it?

How much wine is there?

When can I have it?

What do I need to do today before I start drinking?

Can I walk instead of drive so that I can have a drink?

It's only eleven, I'll have a Valium and a Solpadeine to keep me going for now.

I needed a manageable oblivion. I couldn't cope with the idea of losing control and risking the things I'd worked so hard for: my marriage, my babies, my career, my home. I needed a socially acceptable destruction, which was fine; there was one available to me and it worked well for a while.

At first, the glass of wine in the evening or the vodka tonic in the bath was the epitome of millennial therapy. A socially sanctioned act of self-care: my god-given right and reward as a high-achieving, fully functioning adult woman. As long as I had a book to read and a scented candle lit, the dwindling portions of tonic giving way to straight vodka in my glass didn't matter.

Tweak the image somewhat and society's perceptions shift. If the woman in the bath is unemployed, say, this self-care becomes viewed as lazy and shameful; a similar shift happens when the intention behind the wine in the bath shifts from indulgence to need. Now I am a woman who is lying in the bath soaking in fragrant water and drenched in ethanol, not as some hard-earned treat but out of pitiable desperation. I didn't see this subtle shift from want to need until it was too late. The evolution of my drinking was insidious. Though my appetite for alcohol had always seemed intense, it didn't encroach on my life until suddenly, one day, it did.

Being a so-called high-functioning alcoholic is like starting a fire in your house and then devoting all your energy to preventing its spread: every day you try to keep it from ripping through the rooms and devouring your family. I was dedicated to managing the inferno. It was an exhausting, unending exertion. A cycle of hangovers, inebriation and shame that never resulted in any tangible change, only a continued, just barely contained, illusion of normality. My babies played among the flames and my relationship choked and asphyxiated in the oppressive atmosphere of secrecy, defensive clipped explanations and simmering panic.

The obsession/possession began to control me and little by little I broke my own rules. I began to do the things that once, from a distance, had seemed unthinkable and beyond anything I would be capable of.

The rules were: I wouldn't drink before six, or hide evidence. I wouldn't vomit or drink through a hangover or die of shame. I wouldn't stash and lie and deceive. I wouldn't endanger my babies. But as time passed, I checked every one of those off the list with a grim inevitability. The obsession drove me on through hollow dismal nights drinking on the couch when I was alone and, as I saw it, 'free'. Free to do what I needed to do. After a certain point, I didn't like drinking with other people. There are some people who need the party to conceal their obsession, but my drinking was out of place, even among the drinking of others. It became simply tiresome to drink with other people when I would need to constantly keep myself in check.

I could never quite satisfy my needs in the company of other people because they would've been disgusted by what unfolded in me: the alcohol blurred me until I was just a messy smear of a person, unrecognisable to the people who loved me.

I recognised me though.

When I saw myself drunk in the mirror or in pictures, I never got any jolt of confusion at who this woman was. She embodied everything I knew to be true about myself: needy, greedy, repulsive and pathetic.

If I step just outside of myself for a moment and regard this speedy decent into alcoholism, I can be only awed by the sheer efficiency of the thing. After a long stretch of abstinence in my twenties after the breakdown, I had returned to wine at twenty-seven in time for unexpected motherhood, that most natural of disasters. I drank for six years with increasing thirst until, shaken and ruined, I had my last drink just after my thirty-third birthday. Six years to annihilate myself.

I plummeted in plain sight, but it was against a backdrop of such chaos, I couldn't blame anyone for not seeing it. In those six years, I had two babies, began a new career and lost my father. I was stretched taut between two opposing but equally powerful states: the wild, raw elation that comes with reproducing and the blank, emptiness of delayed grief, the kind that is coiled waiting but has not hit yet. I needed the alcohol to get me up and wind me down in those years. I consoled and coaxed myself through every day of boredom, beauty and pain with the promise of wine. Living was like crawling on skinned knees and only the alcohol could provide any respite.

Why was it all so damn hard? Because I was weak and pathetic? Ungrateful? A shit mother? All of the above? Maybe just born an alcoholic?

When I'd try to persuade myself of the good things I was so lucky to have, my mind devoured itself – the fact that I couldn't seem to feel grateful was confirmation of what a shitty person I was. It was a toxic private life. I hoarded Valium and paid cash in pubs during the daytime so my husband couldn't see the 'cheeky' (as I sold it to myself) lunchtime wines or afternoon G&Ts. I was committed to seeming fine and normal. I definitely didn't mope. Instead I insisted on a punishing schedule – work, gym, running, more work, socialising – made all the more gruelling because of the sheer work my addiction was becoming.

Being a new mum is fucking intense as it is: the entire terrain of your life is no longer recognisable. The first months were bleak. I was perched permanently on the precipice of completely losing it, knowing that tumbling off simply could not be an option: the baby needed feeding, changing, winding, rocking, soothing, everything. Everything. That's an exhausting existence. Being so very, very frightened all the time is exhausting. Having a shower is exhausting. Having a tiny, dark-eyed stranger clinging to you as the hands spin around the clock and the days last forever is exhausting. Trying to pretend not only that you are fine, but happy, truly thrilled and ecstatic, is exhausting.

Now add the hectic *admin* of alcoholism to that equation. Being an addict and keeping track of your shit is a goddamn full-time job. Between sterilising bottles and hiding bottles, the struggle is real, my pals. I'd boast about my powers of multi-tasking here if it wasn't such a toxic brag.

Though in one way, alcoholism and early motherhood were strangely well-suited. I had no routine, no colleagues or friends around to notice any new, concerning behaviours. Also I soon found that there is barely any social cohort as welcoming and tolerant of alcoholic behaviours as the mums on the internet. The mummy wine memes were a balm to my soul every night as I'd hit the finish line of the day and open a bottle of wine.

The memes didn't explicitly say 'sure … every "mama" downs the first glass in one, still standing at the counter in the kitchen while almost crying from relief' but I could fill in the blanks. I deserved this. I needed it. All us 'hero mamas', as we are often called on social media, deserve it. And it's normal. Motherhood is hard. We deserve our glass of 'mummy juice'.

And yeah, fine, I know I don't get to vilify the wine o'clock memes because they're not intended for the likes of me. I was not a woman calmly and casually sipping a sauvignon at the end of a glorious day of peek-a-boo and mummy-baby bonding time, planning our next excursion to the park or baby yoga. I was a woman locked into a continuous internal stream of calculations. *How much wine gone will be noticeable to him when he comes home? I could finish it completely, open a new one and pour one glass and then he'd think I'd only just started? Or switch to a G&T, less obvious that way?*

Still, though not intended to rationalise an alcoholic, mummy wine memes were useful to me. Like my sick dad, I used them as ironclad justification. Parenting sober is just too hard: even the internet agrees. I'd get shit-faced at brunch because Friday nights out were such a rarity – it didn't matter that I drank just as much on a Friday night at home now. Or on a Tuesday, for that matter. No one noticed.

Now that I don't drink at all, it is laughably obvious. Our glass bottle recycling needs are virtually non-existent now, where once the counter by the sink was always crowded – and those were just the ones I didn't hide. Plus there was a lot of Solpadeine cranking me through every murky morning when I snarled at my babies and loathed myself. I do marvel at the force of will that level of drinking, while also maintaining some semblance of normality, took. No wonder I was so wrecked by the end of the drinking days. It was verging on aerobic.

In the last days of my drinking, the obsession drove me. I was never fully present in any given moment, always thinking ahead to my next soothing glass. In many ways, I probably could've continued on a physical level but it was the total psychological takeover that became so unbearable. The drinking edged me out of my own body and onto the peripheries of my own life. It was a huge, growing parasite on my brain, dwarfing every other concern. It possessed me entirely and eventually became bigger than me, something other. It was my rotten baby. It clung to me and it needed me because I was its protection. I sipped wine at the table and watched as it played alongside my matching blond boys. Its rank breath disturbed their blond curls and I shivered at its proximity to them. I couldn't let it hurt them and the only way to prevent that was to nurse it and cosset it and give in to its every whimper and demand. If I deprived it or rejected it, I felt the fallout would destroy my family and ultimately expose my problem.

Exposing the problem is every addict's fear. It's not exactly the shame and humiliation of being found out, though that too is horrendous – it's more the fact that exposure will, one way or another, inevitably result in cutting off the oxygen supply. The unswerving instinct to protect the addiction is like a dark twin of maternal instinct. As long as I minded it like another child, it would be appeased.

Eventually the time comes when there is nothing more important than the rotten baby. It comes before everything. I was willing to be ashamed every single day rather than admit to the problem of this demanding, shrieking baby. I was ready to eviscerate anyone who questioned my drinking – not something that came up all that much, but when it did I could be vicious.

One day near the end of the drinking, my husband asked how much alcohol I'd had and I cringed. Then I flung it all at him: the pain of my comfortable, privileged existence; my grief; my mental illness. The full arsenal of excuses that I always had to hand.

It didn't come up again for a long time, not until we went away with friends for a few days one Easter. Such close proximity to other people was tricky. I got drunker every night, but kept it together. Just.

The tell was when my husband lost it with me one morning after a heavy night. Clearly the pressure of his two small boys and his drunk wife was taking its toll. My friend was shocked. She didn't realise what she was looking at. She didn't see that this was not a disproportionate rage on his part, but a cumulative one that had been mounting in the previous months as I'd begun to lose control of myself and of the situation.

I was manipulative. I let it look like he was completely overreacting. It was Easter, and we got on with the egg hunt we were doing for our older son. I had, in a blackout the night before, scrawled a set of illegible rhyming clues for the hunt. It was pitiful. I saw myself, alone, spread like a stain across the wooden table in the kitchen after the others were asleep. I grappled with the children's colours, trying so hard to complete this act of normality: a mother making a surprise for her child. But I was incapable. The words I'd written to delight my son were mangled by the obsession. It had taken over and was permeating every good thing. I found the illegible clues in the morning and was sickened. They were wretched nonsense. I tore them into pieces, relieved that in the dark of my drunkenness, I'd at least had the wherewithal – or self-preservation really – to not leave them out in view of the others. Of course, even this impulse was a selfish one, done to avoid any questions, done only to protect me and to protect my rancid baby.

It takes a long time for our addiction to turn on us. For years, the addiction is our greatest ally, our only real friend; the thing that will get us through. Before it starts to kill us, it is the only thing helping us survive.

The last weeks were the bleakest. I broke all my rules; the drinking hit a new track. Gone was any self-deception of the glass of wine being a treat or indulgence. It was medicine that had to be taken to reach the required state of numbness. But the thing was, as I came to realise, there was no end to this consuming. This much-desired state of numbness, of fullness, was a horizon that kept on shifting. For many years, I'd had a level I would hit when drinking when I was sated, but this bottom seemed to drop further and further out of reach until by the end it was no longer a vessel I was filling with wine and vodka. Instead I was pitching the glass straight back down my neck and into something infinite. I'd mistakenly believed that all I needed to do was fill this thing and I would eventually be quenched. It was slowly dawning on me that there would never be enough of this for me. The more I poured into me, the greater the chasm grew. I couldn't touch the bottom of this appetite; it simply went on and on. It was a knackering revelation. I will never be done with this, I realised. There will never be enough.

I didn't know what to do with this terrible new information. Where once my mouth had laughed and tasted delicious food and kissed my babies and whispered love in the dark to my husband, now it only drank. It was a drain. When I read the children's bedtime stories, the words swam out, buoyed on cloying wine-heavy breath. As I leaned down to their delicate temples, where fine hair met almost translucent skin, a spidery network of blue veins murmuring just below the surface, I felt I was murdering them. I couldn't kiss them. I didn't deserve to. Instead I tried not to soil them with my obsession and self-pity. I turned away from their clean, warm bodies, and went back down to the open wine on the counter, the thing that would give me respite from the guilty feelings or any feelings at all.

On nights that my husband wasn't there I was relieved. I didn't have to pretend to be anything other than an alcoholic. I didn't have to pretend I was anything other than completely owned by this situation. I was able to get on with this project of mine: finding the bottom. On a Friday night, my timeline would flood with snaps of wine on the couch from mothers I follow. I added my own one, pleased to have some filter to put on this pathological obsession that gave it the veneer of normality.

#Deserved said the pictures of wine. #MamaNeedsWine they crowed. I posted my own glass of white.

'Never needed this more!!!' I typed.

Not pictured: the full bottle I've already finished and the swamp of addiction I'm mired in.

I played with quantities on these solitary nights. I felt sure there was a formula, that with a little experimentation, I would get it right – the exact right ratios of wine to vodka tonic, to food to solitude – that would result in some imagined state of ease and comfort. So often I was held back by the presence of my husband, or the sleeping bodies upstairs. The 'what if' scenarios. What if he comes home and finds me? What if they wake and need me?

On my last night of drinking, I just let go. I got to the 'fuck it' edge and I just jumped. Seb was away. I did my duties: I bathed the babies, vodka tonic in hand – less tonic more vodka. I hissed the words of *Peter Rabbit*, my mind downstairs where my other baby waited. Back downstairs, I was determined. I set myself up on the couch and began. I embarked on the drinking that night with no more pretence. It was liberating at first. I would find the bottom of this thing. I would touch the edge of it and find out where it ended. I was going to jump.

I didn't count on the fact that I would keep on falling. There was no ground to hit. No side or edges to touch, no end to the thirst. I sprawled on the couch in my lovely home, in my lovely life, and kept on pouring. I was dogged. Or *it* was. I was relentless. *It* was relentless. I was in the grip of something that was never going to let me go. It would never leave me alone. This thing would never be done with me.

I never made it to bed that night. I sprawled on the couch, sodden with booze, my mind clogged and filled to capacity with petrol-shop wine, my body gorged but still somehow empty. I made it through three bottles, mostly in a blackout. Maybe the babies cried out for me in the night, I don't know.

Those are blank hours, hours in which my life teetered towards an unknown disaster. I was suspended, drugged and immobilised while potential catastrophe loomed. Nothing disturbed me in this catatonic state. I play the tape of near-misses in my mind as penance. My toddling, trusting baby pitches head first down the stairs and I don't stir. An errant cord nooses round his delicate neck and I don't even know – I'm too ruined with booze to be roused by the muffled whimper of tragedy upstairs. Even holding the babies now, years later, I am trying to comfort those unheard cries, but I never will.

They survived my obsession. I don't deserve this. I deserve to have been dealt the worst. The very worst. But somehow I wasn't. We all survived. So far. Touch wood. Please god. Please please please.

I can't relax into a cosy afterlife of recovery, because this drunk mother is me. She is not a person I can leave behind. I can't graduate from her through time or healing or therapy or the Twelve Steps. The second I forget her is the second my babies are no longer safe. If I think that I have changed or that I am somehow different, then I am as good as adding bleach to their bedtime milk or leaving them wandering alone on a cliff's edge.

Even just writing about the addled years of their babyhood when I was soaked in wine and grief feels dangerous. *I* deserve to be exposed in this way, but them? I'm not sure.

The particularly Irish threat of 'people will talk' hangs heavy over this part of the story. They will be the boys with the drunk mother. Whatever happens to them it will be, 'No wonder, do you not know about the mother?' Even if they excel, it will be viewed through the prism of 'and all that in spite of the mother'. The drunk mother. I cringe at the idea that they will one day read how I bathed them drunk and closed one eye to better focus on Dr Seuss at bedtime. *Oh the places you'll go* (and leave me behind). They'll hate me for this, I'm positive. And I will deserve that. It will be the delayed retribution that I deserve. The delayed retribution that maybe I even need.

I don't know how else to atone for what I have done to them. In a way, them hating me seems like it could be easier, more appropriate than their current sweet well-spring of love. Right now I bask in their outpouring of kisses and cuddles and it feels like I am on the run. I am getting away with something. When they hate me maybe it'll be easier. I won't feel so vile and undeserving.

Committing this to record is an act of insurance on my part. A living declaration: I am an alcoholic, a liar and a manipulator. And I'm good. I'll convince you that I am fine. Fine. Fine. Fine. I'll give you my whole shtick but if you see me and I am blurred and smeared by alcohol don't listen to my cheery lies; I am drowning. I am being hounded by the obsession once more and my babies are not safe.

EPIPHANIES

I first asked the internet if I was an alcoholic in 2014. I was hungover. Googling 'am I an alcoholic' while hungover is a fairly bad buzz, so before I could read the conclusion I deleted the search and the history for safety, and resumed my marathon of carbs and TV, and the marathon work of pretending there was nothing wrong.

At that stage, I had only really begun a tentative foray back to the world of drinking after the lost years of my breakdown when my brain was frenzied and demented enough without introducing any external stimulants. However, when we moved back to Dublin in 2012, I accepted a small glass of wine at a dinner party and so began a decline, though one I didn't detect initially. I had my first child and then my second and because there were periods of abstaining (pregnancy) and because my life was furnished with the expected things (work and friends and family), it was possible to believe that I was a normal drinker. It was a slow slide until suddenly it was a speed descent. The change felt abrupt and out of my control. Need had overthrown want. The last year of my drinking wrecked me.

In the end, I didn't need a list of questions on the internet: I am an alcoholic. At first in the spring of 2018, finally admitting this fact felt experimental. I'd spent so long hiding my addiction that to out it was unthinkable. I started to go about sobriety with all the stealth and duplicitousness that I'd applied to my drinking. It was an exit strategy. If this sober thing didn't work, no harm no foul and I could go back to my cosy life as an alcoholic and people could resume being quietly concerned but the important thing was that I had never, ever admitted it.

The first week of sobriety posed no issue because Seb was away and therefore I could not drink without attracting attention. In the back of my mind were formless thoughts about recovery programs and the Twelve Steps, but I didn't feel ready yet. Instead I listened to a podcast called *Home* recorded by two young women who talked about their drinking and getting sober. One of them, a writer called Laura McKeown, spoke often about how she felt 'we were the lucky ones'. I didn't feel lucky yet. I felt vulnerable and flayed. I was also still swinging back and forth about my embarrassing little penchant for nursing Solpadeines throughout the day.

As each day followed another, I felt genuine amazement that there behind me was another day without alcohol. The sheer novelty of it buoyed me through the first week. I got into bed at night and felt untainted by booze. In the mornings, I woke free and unsullied by fresh shame. It was a rush to dismantle the denial I'd been operating within for so many years, to simply be honest with myself. The intellectual contortions required to be an alcoholic and hide that knowledge from yourself, never mind others, are bleak but impressive, though the constant daily justifications and refrain of *I deserve this, I want this, I need this* are wearing.

When Seb returned from his trip, I was casual about not drinking and he accepted this. I began to toy with a recovery program when the initial honeymoon period of sobriety was punctured by very tangible elements of withdrawal. The things that my wine had masked were starting to come for me. The anxiety, powerful mood swings, the bouts of self-harm invaded. They were all things I'd previously treated with alcohol. I began to accept that I needed more than to simply stop drinking.

I had family who were sober, and it speaks to the power of denial that I'd never once drawn a connection between my own habits and the fact so many close relatives were sober and in the programme. I located a meeting and made provisions to attend secretly on a Saturday morning. I have the kind of job where I would often be going to 'meetings' and not necessarily during the customary hours of business, so Seb didn't enquire further about what I was doing.

The first meeting was awful. I was unbearably millennial about it. I cried all the way through, made it all about me and barely managed to choke out the requisite greeting. 'My name is Sophie and I'm an alcoholic.'

It's interesting that this greeting has infiltrated common parlance and is a tired set-up for lazy jokes and jaded lifestyle journalists. I'm certain I've used it in desperation once or twice. 'My name is Sophie and I'm a Belieber,' that kind of thing. Its casual utterance has neutered it to some extent. We say it with little thought to the impact it can have when sitting in a room of compassionate strangers and for the first time acknowledging something that most likely you have strenuously worked to deny every day until that point. It is momentous.

Before I'd entered that room, I remember imploring the unknown entity I occasionally beg for help in finding my keys and the like for there to be just one person that looked like me in there. I thought I needed a woman near my own age, someone to identify with. In fact, I didn't need this. I learned fairly quickly that the terrain of addiction is surprisingly universal. In the years since that day, I have listened to middle-aged businessmen and men who've been in prison and women in their eighties all describe in minute detail exactly what it feels in my head and in my body.

The book written by the founders of the programme is also full of familiar passages I could've written, despite it being a nearly ninety-year-old text peppered with the occasional dated and irritating generalisations about women that one might expect from a document of that era. It's uncanny.

After the first meeting, a woman I vaguely knew came up to me. She patiently listened to my nervy patter and reassured me about some things mentioned at the meeting that were giving me pause – namely god or a higher power.

'Don't get too hung up on all that if you can. Lots of people are very take-it-or-leave-it about that part. Some people make their children their higher power or the people in the rooms. Hitch it to whatever you think will help you stay sober.' A week from then, Kev would be dead one year. It seemed a handy coincidence. I decided I'd think of him any time a higher power was mentioned. The woman I vaguely knew gave me her number and a hug.

Leaving I remember thinking, *Ah Dublin! Of course I knew someone there*, but since then the constellation of synchronicities that have accompanied my recovery have forced me to acknowledge the intangible power I'm convinced is at play.

Spirituality is not something I'd engaged with much before. My family's religion is gossip. They agree with the message 'do unto others as you would have them do unto you' – what's not to like? But given the religious institutions themselves appear to struggle with this basic tenet and given the harm perpetrated by religious organisations particularly in this country, my parents didn't engage.

'Just keep following the signs,' the woman from the meeting had told me. I took this literally, as each meeting room is littered with signs spouting aphorisms like 'one day at a time' and 'easy does it', but as the weeks of sitting in rooms in church basements, community centres and hospitals drifted by, I felt a persistent sense that the path of recovery was being illuminated either through the people I met or the things I heard being shared. Coincidences abound in the rooms. And the honesty and compassion in these spaces creates a palpable power of its own.

In the early weeks, I was jangly with chronic anxiety. For that spring and much of the summer, I battled a kind of nausea of the mind and vibrated with an unpleasant restlessness. It exposed the emotional precariousness that I'd been subduing with booze. Still, I was sleeping better, and no longer trudging through my perma-hangover, however, I was exhausted by how full-on my new unmediated existence felt with nothing to blunt the edges. *Jesus*, I'd think. *Sober people are the real ballers. We're out here raw-dogging reality every day.*

I'd misheard people in the rooms talk about 'piece of mind' and I seized on it. That's exactly how I felt, like my mind was in pieces. Ironically I'd been coping better in my drinking days. I'd been robustly ploughing through my work, hitting deadlines, raising my kids, doggedly pursuing the ambitions I was addicted to as much as booze, showing up for my life, and consuming whatever it took to numb myself out in any given moment. I'd been fucking *nailing* everything in my alcoholism – now I was a shaky, quaking mess trying to fit pieces of a frayed mind back together.

Then it hit me. *They're saying 'peace of mind'!* I nearly laughed out loud in the meeting when I realised this for the first time. I feel like 'peace' was such a distant concept for me at that moment that I hadn't even put this together.

And 'peace of mind' is probably mentioned at least once in every single meeting so it actually took some mental effort to continuously recast it as 'piece of mind' in my head. Of course understanding it didn't bring it to me, but it gave me a sense of what all this sharing and facing things was steering me towards.

After about eight weeks, I decided to tell some people about my tenuous sobriety. It seemed like a good safety net to put in place. I wanted to tell people so that it would make me accountable. I sensed it would also help me commit to recovery, because the thing that was holding me back was the part of me that still truly couldn't quite accept I was an alcoholic. I was phobic about drinking in the here and now. I frequently had dreams in which I drank alcohol and woke up as though from a nightmare. I didn't want to drink, it held real trauma for me. It still does.

However, the diseased part of me didn't let up. *So you're never drinking again? You'll never enjoy a cold glass of white wine in the sun in the garden when you're retired?* It was such an odd fantasy to latch on to. For some reason, I was acting like Seb and I would be retiring to the British reality TV show *Escape to the Chateau.* And not only that, but I was concerned that I'd have to tolerate this distant hypothetical situation completely sober. Plus this fantasy was based on a completely false argument: that my drinking was ever that pleasant or civilised to begin with. Far more likely a scenario was ex-pat me, sitting in the garden of the chateau, drinking seven to nine wines, talking copious shite or crying, before vomiting in a bush and being put to bed at 6pm.

I told Seb first during breakfast one Saturday morning.

'I have to go to a meeting today.'

'Cool,' he was reading on his phone.

'I have to tell you something.'

'Oh?'

'The meetings I go to – well, some, not all – they're recovery meetings. For alcoholism. Because I'm an alcoholic.'

Seb has yet to be shocked by anything in the fifteen years I've known him and this was no different. Outwardly, he seemed to barely register what I'd just said.

'Okay, cool,' he said.

Since then we have on occasion talked more deeply about it and he has probed a little. Maybe he wasn't shocked, because when you live with an alcoholic, even one as secretive and careful as I was, you fucking know that you live with an alcoholic.

Also when your marriage contains a secret, any secret, that secret creates a noxious atmosphere, permeating everything and disrupting the harmony. Even if only one person knows, the secret is there mushrooming between you both in bed at night or side by side watching Netflix. The secret still tips off the innocent party, arousing their anxiety with its hidden destructive potential. I am still pursued by a jumble of half-remembered confrontations between us, him angry and disgusted, me drunk and contemptible. I still can hear him saying reproachful but utterly valid things during those times and I can't believe he stayed with me. He says now that he was just too lazy to leave, and thank god for that. And thank god he can make jokes about it.

Telling my mother took longer. I don't know why exactly. She has had a degree of proximity to this affliction herself. She would certainly be understanding. And I had been sober a few months by then and gaining clarity every day. Maybe part of my reluctance was presenting yet another genre of my self-replenishing dysfunction to her: '*Sophie is a fuck-up* now comes in Alcoholic Flavour!' That sort of thing.

I told her in her kitchen one Sunday morning out of the blue. I myself hadn't anticipated the information tumbling out in the middle of our morning coffee, never mind my poor mother. She took it remarkably well. My mother is one of life's great over-reactors, but almost exclusively reserves her overreacting for only the most minor of issues. If, for example, I had told her that morning that I'd gotten a taxi to her house she would've hit the roof. It would have galled her on so many levels: the waste of money – 'I could've picked you up!' – the illogic of it – 'But you live five minutes' walk away!' – and these thoughts would have probably eaten her alive all day and into the night until 3am when she would sit bolt upright in her bed and text me:

> I've been thinking about the taxi you got earlier. Why don't you bring one of your dresses down to the designer consignment store and they can sell it to replace the €5 you wasted on that taxi earlier?

Regarding my alcoholism, she was notably calm. We didn't do the full run-down of it then and there. We hugged. She acknowledged obliquely that it ran in the family as it does in most Irish families and we got on with the coffee and gossip. In the months after, she'd occasionally

230

ask harder questions but she's been incredibly non-judgmental about it. Impressively so.

In the rooms, we talk a lot about how the programme teaches us how to live. When I think of my drinking life, I'm always struck by what a confining existence it was. I had lots of the outward elements of a 'successful' person. But my drinking was a severe hindrance. It stymied friendships and blighted my perspective until I was completely tunnel-visioned. I saw no value in anything except in respect to alcohol. A day at the beach was pointless without beers in the picnic bag. A night in? Unthinkable without wine. Driving to meet friends? Absolutely not – why bother when you couldn't drink? These were things connected to my alcoholism that I'd never noticed before.

I'd existed in such a crappy, shrunken world when the addiction was in full flight that when it was extracted little by little I genuinely had a sense of needing to learn, at age thirty-three, just what it is that people actually *do* with their lives.

Predictably, in the first six months of sobriety, I tried initially to latch my addictive nature to work and exercise. I worked and ran compulsively, because compulsive doing can induce a numbing state: it eats the hours, provides escape and prevents us from having to think too much. However, manic productivity – such a reassuring state – was not what I needed. I needed a rest and when I didn't comply, my brain said: ''K, if you're going to be a lunatic about this, I'll *make* you rest' and gifted me an episode of acute mental illness. Thanks, brain!

Eventually I began to try things in moderation. I went to a so-called Casual Choir where, for two hours, 150 people got together to learn an arrangement of a popular song. I loved it, and marvelled at the fact that a year ago I wouldn't have ever thought to go, it not being an obvious opportunity for drinking. Or I'd have gone and turned it into one.

It makes me sad to think of all the things and people I rejected in favour of my addiction. In the rooms, I try to release the sadness and the shame of my drinking years. I am not an alcoholic who buys wholesale into the idea that I have a disease. I believe it to be more complex than that. And I can't stop blaming myself. I can't shake it: my alcoholism was something that I perpetrated on my loved ones. I carry a lot of grief around my drinking. For merging something so toxic with my children's baby years. But I am trying to learn self-compassion.

Towards the end of the first year in the programme, epiphanies rained on me. People I already knew strayed across my path in the recovery rooms. I began to feel the magic that comes from such basic and straightforward things as acceptance, honesty and faith. At the beginning I had struggled with the concept of faith and effectively ducked the higher power question, feeling unready to de-centre myself as faith requires.

I listened as people, over and over, shared their own antipathy toward god or a higher power and I heard others talk about the simple act of getting down on your knees and praying. Even though I'd done everything else that was suggested to me, I resisted the praying, I think, because I didn't really understand it.

'Just follow the signs,' the woman had said.

Since she'd spoken those words, I had not had a drink. What bigger sign did I need that something here was working? Whether it's a sign on the wall or something even more ephemeral, a numinous quality that's created when people come together to speak and be vulnerable?

I once saw a slogan on a yoga brand t-shirt that really pissed me off: 'You'll see it when you believe it.' *Oh fuck off*, I thought at the time. But now I think it's not a bad inspo quote, if we're insisting on an inspo quote and I suppose I am, in this instance.

What I take from it is this: no one can prescribe faith or spirituality to you. Only you can appoint your system of beliefs. In the rooms, 'god', when mentioned, is described always in the same terms: a god of our understanding. It's clever – it alienates only the most pedantic people who bridle even just at the use of the g-word. A god of our understanding acknowledges the broadness of human faith.

In the rooms, I began to feel lucky. The text promised that I would know a new freedom, and I do. Sometimes people ask if I feel amazing because I don't drink. They don't know that I'm an alcoholic, they just mean in a more general way, I presume, but when you've come from alcoholic drinking into sobriety, the only word for it is freedom.

Sometimes, people say well done for giving up, and I always feel weird accepting this praise, because in the end it didn't feel like a choice; it was an imperative, a bid for survival. Plus the whole thing feels like it was taken out of my hands somehow. It certainly wasn't through will power. Will power had not worked for me. Back in my drinking days, I could've barely will-powered my way through a single day without drinking, never mind the 900 or so I have since then.

On the subject of praying, I eventually said, *What the hell? Why do I think I'm above praying? I'm a fucking gross alcoholic.* Of course there's many ways to get sober and faith is not a prerequisite. But my god, it helped me and I am so grateful for every sober hour I get. I was so grateful, then and now, that eventually it seemed churlish to not say thank you. So I got down on my knees as had been repeatedly suggested. And I prayed to a god of my understanding.

When I try to analyse my faith, I find it is impossible to articulate in a satisfactory way. I suppose because it is mysterious. Why and how does it work? I don't know how; I only know that the obsession lifted and has stayed gone since I started to believe. In the end, it was a bit of a chicken-egg thing. I started to have faith because I had proof: the proof was me, still sober and free. Still sober and free because I have faith.

As the annoying t-shirt says: I see it because I believe it.

PART 4
HEREDITARY

BAD TIMING

For a week in July, there's a life stirring at the centre of my own. It is hidden but persistently there somehow. Like my other two babies before it, I feel it tugging deep in me. I can even feel which ovary is the culprit – the right, I'm sure of it. I tolerate the nausea washing in and out several times a day. My nausea with this one is tidal: when it recedes for brief spells, there still lingers a fishy garbage flavour at the back of my throat.

On the first day, I buy the test to reassure myself that my wild mood and grinding, twisting cramps are merely garden-variety womanhood and not something far more seismic. I opt to piss on this little divining rod in the bathroom of my younger son's crèche. This might seem an odd location but probably not to anyone who's raised kids.

Moments to yourself are snatched from your children's lives and secreted selfishly away. I know I am not pregnant; I am just reassuring myself. Just killing this niggling little question mark. I sit, knickers at my knees, flicking from app to app on my phone, unable to be in this moment too completely. It's not even possible, I repeat. It's not.

It is.

'I'm having a panic attack,' I type to my friend.

'Do you want me to ring you?'

'Yes in two minutes please.' I have to get my son. I stagger to standing and sway with the out-of-body feeling that only a shock this potent inspires. I am listing. I am untethered. I know this feeling. My babies are the kind that creep up on you apparently. I am thirty-four; it's not like when I was younger. With my eldest, the day I took the test and found out I was pregnant I was paralysed with shock, but there was a freedom in being young and clueless. I had nothing to lose and no idea what was coming.

This time I am thirty-four and people rely on me. A chill now drifts through my body and down my arms to the tips of my fingers. Severe anxiety. In this moment, this crouching cluster of cells feels like a threat. What impact will it have on my life? And the lives of those I love?

'Text when ready. This will pass,' she writes.

'I don't know about that,' I respond.

I hide the test and slip out into the hall where children are swarming. *Of all the places to be having a crisis pregnancy.* I dodge around them as if touching them could make me even more pregnant. I make for my son's door and am immediately winded by his hug. That's when the guilt sees her moment and grips me, ushering in a new era of self-loathing.

In my real life, I am staunchly pro-choice. I actively campaigned like so many friends and was so relieved when the country came out in support of repealing the eighth amendment in 2018. Since the nineteenth century, abortion had been a criminal offense in Ireland and in the 1980s an amendment had been made that gave a foetus equal rights as the mother who carried it. As predicted, it played out in practice with tragic results: a traumatised fourteen-year-old girl forced to petition the high court for the right to travel for a termination, countless women being exiled to Britain to obtain this care and eventually the death of Savita Halappanavar, who was denied an abortion as she suffered a complicated miscarriage and died as a result.

However, hours into my new life as a pregnant mother-of-two, I learned that there is one abortion that I am against: my own. I didn't think I could handle another baby but growing up in a place that rated the life of a cluster of cells as on a par with the life of a living woman has its effects. I couldn't shake the guilt. For other women this essential healthcare was their right. For me it was a selfish act remedying something I had brought on myself through carelessness and stupidity. *This is all your own fault. You were obviously being careless. You must've fucked up the contraception. Bad timing is not a good enough reason.* And for this mishap, apparently, I will have another baby.

I step outside of this ceaseless internal monologue momentarily to simply admire the efficiency of misogyny. *Oh you're good! Give us a constitution that devalues our very lives. Feed us enough fucked-up messaging and we'll just cut out the middleman and shame and repress ourselves.* There are no good or bad abortions, this is a fact. I know this. I wheel my bike through the July sun, holding the soft clammy hand of my baby boy who stops every few paces to examine and name the things he sees. While my friend, on speaker phone, repeats soothing, sensible things down the line.

'This is why we have abortion. This will be okay. You don't have to decide anything today.'

Her words don't break stride, even as I periodically talk baby nonsense back to my son to appease his toddler echolalia. My friend and I are each used to having every calibre of life talk while ducking and diving and weaving around our children. Death, divorce and gossip all have been punctuated by exclamations of 'oh, yes it is an aeroplane' and 'oh now, the mean old door banged the baby' as the children rush like coursing rapids around our solid mother selves.

My illogical fear ricochets from unfounded concern to unfounded concern. What if I am the only woman who abortions don't work on? What if Seb tries to stop me having one? What if I have the baby and it unravels me completely? What if I never come back from it?

The thoughts are as they sound: illogical. They are quite literally ill logic: panicked what-ifs I use to torture myself.

· · ·

Weeks have passed and I am still possessed by this thing, the cluster, but I am not engaging. Seb and I have a tacit agreement not to refer to the monumental invisible new presence in our lives. We don't use the word 'baby' and instead refer to it only in the most oblique terms. We are putting off making a decision, because who wants to make that decision? I am at sea night and day with this thing. It's taken over me like no pregnancy before ever did. A part of my resolve to not engage is pretending that I am not fucked and dog-tired with it. I am trudging on through tasks and obligations as though nothing at all is wrenching at me.

My days are spent doggedly searching for the one bite of something that will appease the nausea brought on by this belligerent entity. I pick up and put down things all day long. What works one day will not necessarily the next. Chipsticks offer a temporary breather from the nausea, though now, from here in my second month of pregnancy, just typing the words 'chip' and 'stick' have me sucking down air and fighting back the swell of sickness erupting in my stomach. For four consecutive days I frequent the same shelf in the supermarket for Campbell's cream of tomato soup. This oddly neon soup works at first: I dip cream crackers covered with precisely executed egg mayonnaise, and for the duration of the meal I feel mercifully steady. Then as the last bite goes down I look at the remnants with a sudden fresh horror, as though I've come to and found myself feasting on human flesh. 'Jesus Christ, why?' I implore no one in particular.

At this point in pregnancy, 10 per cent of the DNA fragments in my blood are those of the foetus. This accounts for the feeling of invasion I am currently having. It's a bodily takeover, and right now this thing inside me doesn't care that I don't have time to be consumed by new life. I push on through inboxes and pick-ups and drop-offs and deadlines, but I am dragging an unwilling body around on these errands. Even I can sense that giving in is not too far off.

I am working on other stories for this book, but the needy thing in the pit of me won't have it. My focus is shot and eventually I relent and take up these words instead. It serves to prove a point I don't want to think about. How many babies does it take to fell a woman?

My grandmother was a titanic being, unsinkable even after eight squalling, needing, pushing children. But I don't know anything of her life before the inevitability of being a Catholic woman in the fifties and sixties had subsumed her plans. What had she seen for herself? Surely not the commercial quantities of milk, bread, sausages and spuds that, according to my mother, her six brothers ate as effort-lessly and fluidly as they breathed in oxygen.

My mother opted for just the one. And while I'm not certain that this was a master plan, her career evolved to become something that ultimately looked like it wouldn't be that compatible with more children.

What's the cut-off? How many prams in the hall does it take to level our ambition? Funny that Cyril Connolly, a male critic, should be concerned with prams in the hall – no *man's* creative impetus has ever been viewed as compromised by fatherhood, but a mother? That's a different story.

Even lying as I am now, beached and sagging as the couch in my office strains under me, making illegible notes on a heavy afternoon in the listless tenth week of a thing I'm loath to call a thing, I know I have succumbed. I have succumbed physically and, more worryingly, mentally. I gave up the piece of writing I'd been charging at each morning with such fury and instead I have come down with a kind of maternal consumption. I simply cannot summon the will to think about anything else: it's a dastardly trick of biology.

Profound fatigue in early pregnancy is due in part to changes in hormones but what is really happening, I sense, is the body neatly wresting back a woman's borrowed autonomy. Now we exist for the interloper. Make her leaden so she cannot jump on trampolines. Or run to the nearest abortionist. Make her nauseated so she doesn't suddenly go after unpasteurised dairy or deli meats or whatever other delicacy the Americans (they're particularly hysterical on this) have outlawed for gestating women. Even the sore tits speak to some biological carnal inhibiting – keep her neutered and tamed.

At a dinner party years ago, an older woman announced that I'd better do whatever it was I wanted to get done before I came down with children. She had an adult son and an amazing career, but she seemed pissed off. She couldn't have known that at that very moment I was already colonised by the fabulous first boy whose arrival would see me become a near-perfect dolphin impressionist just to solicit his peals of burbling laughter.

She couldn't know because *I* certainly didn't know. I thought I was just intensely raging at everyone and everything. I didn't realise a tangle of something taking root in your body could possess you so instantly and mercilessly. When I did finally wonder about my fits of weeping and fury, not to mention the Findus Crispy Pancakes I was horsing into me, my first son was firmly ensconced. A stranger who, in the mere minutes it took for my piss to sweep up the pregnancy test and reveal a positive line, became the most important person in my life. Maternal consumption.

The woman's words stalked me. 'Do what you want to get done.' What did I want to get done? At twenty-eight, I didn't really know. Despite appearing to have abandoned my creative life after my breakdown six years before, a part of me had hoped I would eventually pick it up again. I was working as a chef, but while I loved my days slinging plates and making good food, I didn't feel any burning desire to prove myself beyond cushy shifts in nice cafés and restaurants. I think it might be why I stayed at it for six years. It was a much safer option than to wade back into art and risk reawakening an ambition that might remain unfulfilled. Ambition is a terrible thing to be struck down with, as consuming as a tiny foetus in many ways.

I didn't want to admit how powerfully I wanted to be a writer. To my mind there were already writers in the family – real ones. I carried on with orders, prep lists, service and the hurly-burly of kitchen life. My belly grew under my apron, and I was busy – which is a very safe state for me. I cannot rest idle for even a moment; it is like the childhood game where the floor is lava, except it is the empty hour which is lava – a gap into which I might stumble, back into a sick mind. It's safer to keep busy. I had tentatively begun to write before the first baby, and began to face the fact that this was what I wanted to do.

After his birth and with the pram in the hall, I waited for the impetus to create to start leaking out of me, as the woman had promised. It seemed likely, especially given everything else that was streaming from my body at that point. Instead, the reverse happened. I held his tiny body, scrawnier and darker than I'd expected, and I felt unworthy. *I have to make something of myself for you. I will*, I promised the tense little thing with the sparrow legs and worried eyes.

I never told the woman that the very opposite of her prediction had come true. That far from sapping me, the baby spurred me. I wrote my first book during his baby-hood. I didn't tell her because I couldn't risk acknowledging it – it felt too precarious. I still fully expected motherhood to hijack me. It wasn't a matter of if but when.

I heard my mother and her friends discussing the women who came back from maternity leave, only to leave again and never return. Like they had pushed their luck and paid the price.

I myself had a conversation with a friend just months before the knotty issue of this third baby had taken root. She is an artist and a mother of two. We were discussing the difficulty of blending these two opposing states: artist and mother.

At the time, I told her I felt I was at maximum capacity in terms of what I could give my children while still having something left in terms of emotional space for my work. Creating of any description requires a degree of isolation that isn't naturally compatible with motherhood. Having children changes you; it's undeniable. They seize your love and they take the position you once afforded your work. Once you have them, there is quite simply nothing above them in the hierarchy of your concerns. As Simone de Beauvoir put it, mothers develop 'fatal patience'. Our lives can wait, our desires slow and our needs stall in the face of our children's.

How much does it cost to be an artist mother?

The artist mother is different to the straight-up working mother, though neither is easier than the other. Each is harshly judged, though the traditional working mother may have clearer economic motivations to excuse her absence in the home. The artist mother is more of a fringe citizen: selfish and work-obsessed without even the excuse of financial imperative to dissuade her detractors from their sighs and shaking heads.

So much of the labour of art is not visible in the final product. The empty hours of day-dreaming and analysis are not accounted for in the finished painting. When it comes to writing, whole swathes of dross need to be written to then be carved away. 'Kill your darlings,' they say of edits in movie-speak. It's a phrase I hate because it reminds me how, Medea-like, my ambitions might be hurting my darlings. When I write at home they come in and out: *I'm not a man, after all; I can't expect awed, unimpeachable respect for my work.* Also I'm proud not to work that way: we don't expect perfect conditions. We write notes in the dark under our sleeping children, we march with babies strapped to our chests and feed them while we dream about the stories we tell.

Still, millennial motherhood is one fraught with knowledge. We are armed with too many studies of child development shared in anxious WhatsApp groups. The non-stop thoughts and opinions of strangers online infiltrate and undermine our own thoughts and opinions while hot takes on the effects of full-time childcare haunt our broken sleep.

Being a mother is to be the root cause of all your child's problems and sole focus of their ire. As Deborah Levy wrote in *The Cost of Living*:

> If she moves beyond us, comes close to being a self that is not at our service, she has transgressed from the mythic, primal task of being our protector. Yet, if she comes too close, she suffocates us … If our mother does the things she needs to do in the world, we feel she has abandoned us. It is a miracle she survives our mixed messages, written in society's most poisoned ink.

Women's liberation has stalled at the border of Mother-Land. Look at the women in harmonious equal relationships, who wake up the day after their first child is born and discover that they now have two children, one a bouncing eight-pounder and one in its mid-thirties of considerable more heft. Regard the rampant concern-trolling of mothers. As a society, we have just, *just*, about grasped that we can no longer openly police what women wear, do, think, say and eat but the minute, the *second*, that woman is fertilised, it is a fucking free-for-all of concerned unsolicited advice ranging from what not to eat, what exercise is 'allowed' and the correct way to look and be and feel in pregnancy.

At a wedding, a woman once intercepted a canapé of pâté just as it was about to enter my mouth when I was six months' pregnant. Just imagine the thought process that led to her to decide that she knew what was best for me, a grown woman, to eat. Imagine for a moment that I saw a woman smoking and thoughtfully strolled over to intercept her. The fact is that pregnancy and then, in turn, the resulting children, gives society a carte blanche to go back to what we love to do best: judge women.

If I sound hysterical just consider the date the eighth amendment to the Irish constitution was repealed. 27 May 2018. It took thirty-four years (not, obviously counting the centuries prior to that) for this country to recognise that women could be trusted with their own bodies.

There is barely a section of society policed more than mothers, and the worst part of all is that it is largely women assiduously tracking and chronicling the crimes and misdemeanours of other women on this front. I have written on difficult subjects before, but nothing gives me pause like wading into the charged waters of motherhood.

Even just writing this essay unnerves me: will it some day be a hostage to fortune because I neglected to put a disclaimer about how much I love my children at the start? Admitting any kind of ambivalence towards motherhood even when directed, in this abstract way, at the institution, the societal concept of motherhood, can prove inflammatory. Anything beyond the party line of gratitude and joy for our children is considered taboo. A man doesn't need to execute these mental and emotional gymnastics to take part in parenthood and his working life, and neither should a woman.

Part of the problem is surely the underlying implication of the 'how does she do it?' narrative – that she won't be doing whatever 'it' is for long once there's a pram in the hall. The general sense is that the woman who is confounding us with how she's doing it is on borrowed time. Because we are the ones compromised by life. All it takes is one more baby or an ailing parent and she is neatly capsized. Men are, for the most part, just not players in this story to the same extent. And of course I'm not saying that men don't love and care for their families with all their being: I'm saying that they're just not expected to in the same way. When a man leaves work to attend to his child, it is commended; when a woman leaves work to attend to her child, it is noted.

As I consider the next pram, I scrounge for examples of women still successfully making their work in the face of three children. I bring the perfect specimen of Late Capitalist Woman Who Has It All to coffee with my mother. Not literally, of course. Don't worry, I don't invite her to sit in silence at the table with us while we debate her choices and achievements. But I hold the fact of her up to my mother for scrutiny.

'Look! Elizabeth is doing it all with three kids in tow.' I petition my mother for some kind of approval.

'Well *you're* not Elizabeth.' These words will turn out to be my mother's downfall.

'What is that supposed to mean?' I'm ready with the indignation.

'Oh nothing, nothing,' she's backtracking, wishing no doubt she could kill off those particular darlings.

'No, you meant something by that. What is it?'

'Well, Elizabeth is just a much more *optimistic* person than you are, Pumpkin.'

I realise this is her way of saying: 'Well, Elizabeth is just a lot less *mentally ill* than you are, Pumpkin.'

I'm momentarily stumped. She's not wrong, to be fair.

Eventually I ask if it's ever occurred to her that given the sheer volume of mental illness I've weathered, that perhaps I am, in fact, a remarkably positive and optimistic person. Maybe even to an annoying extent.

'I should be lauded for putting up with my stupid brain all these years,' I argue.

'Yes, Pumpkin.'

In the end, there was no real question or debate. The shock passed and we rubbed the growing belly that announced itself impertinently just months into the pregnancy. Our oldest christened the bump SpikeTwig and SpikeTwig was welcomed with the kind of brutal affection all younger siblings are born to.

Creating art and life in tandem is new, but maybe more natural than I realised. Being pregnant has slowed me. It's forced me to inhabit the days and moments more fully. Much of this book and the last have been written lying down; the discomfort of sitting at my desk was just too much. The bump has forced me back to bed on many days and I wonder if this is the shape of things to come. Will this baby finally hold me still? In the last few years, my version of having it all involved a life lived at break-neck speed. I accepted every commission; I was frenzied in my work. I took short maternity leaves. I was petrified to say no to anything and consequently every week felt like a scramble. The empty hours are lava, remember. But is it any way to live?

Babies force us to abandon structure. Routines can help us feel a sense of control amid the chaos, but really it's at best an illusion of routine. We are on baby time now. They force us to recalibrate to their timing and their pace.

Each of my babies came with some kind of epiphany. My first gleefully and starkly exposed my immaturity; my second ushered me through the coping years and helped me realise I was an addict. This baby could be the one to teach me of the irrelevance of timing. What is good timing and what is bad timing? Surely I've been a parent long enough by now to know that the surest way to invite the universe to fuck with you is to announce that you have things under control.

And so we await our sweet, impish, badly timed baby and I read back over the words that, in a way, we've written together.

MILK (AND MADNESS)

Mostly my babies stole into being on a mysterious convergence of casual negligence, luck and love. Only one was in any way *pre*-conceived before he was conceived. In these times, when so little is left untracked or unmeasured by one app or another, I enjoy these stowaways. It restores the pleasantly primal aspect of reproducing that was robbed when sense prevailed and planning became possible. Their sudden presence is rarely heralded by any sensible calculation of absent bleeding, but rather a subtle pressure shift inside me. A heady rage usually rushes through me like some hormonal easterly, along with the crampy abdominal tugging of something latching on and digging in. A parasite taking possession of its host.

It still strikes me as a weird way to go about multiplying. 'People don't fit inside people,' I wail to Seb, beached under the latest progeny-to-be. 'If men had to be the ones doing this there's no way man would have ever bothered landing on the moon! Scientists would've been sorting this shitshow out as priority, not dicking around in moon dust.'

From the packaging, millennial motherhood seems just the loveliest, doesn't it? Tasteful pregnancy photo shoots adorn the Instagram grids of celebrities and civilians alike. Women, looking serene, cradling sleeping babies, gazing in adoration at the child, arm presumably raised with iPhone to capture this private moment and spread the implied message: motherhood is the ultimate in female accomplishment. For our grandmothers, motherhood was such a foregone conclusion in the lives of most women as to be hardly worth remarking upon. My mother tells how, in the mid-eighties when she was expecting, it was understood that women like her should do their utmost to conceal their pregnancies and airbrush any trace of motherhood from their professional interactions, lest anyone detect a hint of distraction or decreased interest in career advancement. Now, I wonder at the feverish hard-sell we're receiving via social media feeds. The rose-filtering and fetishising of the experience seemed to directly coincide with women at last gaining some modicum of autonomy over whether or not motherhood would be happening to them. It all seems a bit suspect.

I remember drifting beatifically through the months of my first pregnancy and noticing other mothers giving me conspiratorial glances and nods. I assumed it was some kind of 'welcome to the sisterhood' vibe. Later, after the baby had been born and I'd begun to direct similar looks to young pregnant women, I realised what was actually being silently broadcast:

You poor bitch. You have no idea.

And she doesn't for the most part. How could she? In part of what seems to be a societal conspiracy, no one ever really tells young women what is coming. How can you sum up such an experience, one that will simultaneously be the most disappointing and rewarding of your life? And no other aspect of the human experience is commodified and branded like modern motherhood; it's a system that feels practically engineered to keep women striving and grappling with failure.

The books are no help. For starters, baby books by their very nature are too long. We need a baby pamphlet, bearing just a single sentence: 'It's just a phase.'

The only other sound piece of advice anyone can or should give a pregnant woman is 'lower your expectations'. The worst thing anyone can have wading into this baby-making scenario is high expectations. That's why the false advertising of motherhood is so damaging. It's dangerous to sell any experience as roundly joyous, life-affirming and profoundly altering. Nothing is that good. However, the punishment if women deviate from the party line when it comes to motherhood can be merciless. Women who've voiced even the most minor ambivalence toward their experience are pilloried. Think of Rachel Cusk, who said of her honest and wonderful account of motherhood, *A Life's Work* (2001):

> I was accused of child-hating, of postnatal depression, of shameless greed, of irresponsibility, of pretentiousness, of selfishness, of doom-mongering and, most often, of being too intellectual.

At the time of its publication, reviewers actually said this book should be kept from pregnant women. You see, it *is* a conspiracy!

To pregnant women I say, make a birth plan if it makes you feel good, but accept that you may wind up using that birth plan to clean up your mucus plug off the passenger seat of the car.

Motherhood is, I believe, at its core an ever-shifting power exchange between us and our children. When I became pregnant for the first time, I innocently thought, *Ah, I'm having a baby …* Even though from almost day one that soon-to-be baby brought me to my knees, first with mood swings, then nausea, then stretching pains and so on until I had to admit around week twenty that really it was much more like this baby was having me. Which is a fairly persistent sensation throughout the early years of motherhood. My children still dwell in and around my body; I am swarmed by them in a way that their father is not. My best hope for a moment without full body contact is to stay on the move. They hurl themselves toward me, a slow-moving vessel; they glance off my body, tiny hands caressing unconsciously before they then ricochet off into their play once more. However, if I pause, moor myself anywhere for even just a moment, they are back immediately, circling before scaling me and resuming their petting and pummelling.

As I am currently being devoured from the inside again – another baby is having me – I have had to hold their raucous affection at bay as best I can in case they kick or clamber over the belly too roughly.

With my first baby I was able to give myself wholly over to this colonisation but it's a hard transition to make from being an independent republic to suddenly being occupied. I still worked as a chef at the time and was impatient with the new cumbersome appendage that got in my way around the kitchen. I was also increasingly exhausted and began to look forward to the day when the baby would be out of my body, not understanding that would be a superficial change at best, and unlikely to feel much different. I didn't understand that he would no longer be dwelling *inside* me but would instead be *on* me, crouched and permanently feasting.

I was a long time adjusting to this new, odd life of consuming and being consumed. I remember constantly trying to get away from the baby, not really grasping that, at that point, they simply won't have it. You are their home and their only food source: why would they tolerate you trying to get away?

'She tried to get away,' became a running joke between Seb and I as we contemplated the hostage situation the baby now kept us in. It was a quote from *Dead Man's Shoes,* a brilliantly psychotic revenge film by Shane Meadows. In it Paddy Considine's character stalks and traps a group of men in a house and tortures them. He says the line 'He tried to get away,' in a deeply sinister voice while indicating a victim he has stuffed into a suitcase. Exactly what we always predicted we'd be comparing parenthood to, right?

The first days of motherhood were, for me, more terrifying than some of my worst days of breakdown. I hadn't prepared for the strangeness of it all. Towards the end of the pregnancy, paranoid obsessive thoughts had once more begun to take hold and I had become phobic of the most innocent things, like the tiny baby clothes we'd packed for the hospital and the sweet little hats and blankets. I imagined that on the day of his birth when I was gutted of him, along with his strangled cries filling the room some virus was unleashed and infected me for the year that followed. I was too scared to admit how scared I was and instead applied myself to the motions of motherhood with a fever that bordered on pathological: again maternal consumption.

My experience of breastfeeding the first time was a potent cocktail of awe and misery. I had not anticipated that something so natural as feeding your baby could feel so profoundly disappointing. Why couldn't I get it? Why didn't I have enough milk for him? And why did this fact hurt on such a visceral level? The ongoing feeding issues wore away at my already compromised resilience. No sleep, the druggie hangover of my C-section and the shadow of old breakdown feelings meant I began to sink. However, the maternal consumption meant I couldn't conceive of 'giving in' and admitting I wasn't well. Instead, I began a committed approximation of the motherhood I saw around me. It was a grotesque pantomime: I'd cry in the shower in the mornings, allowing only the most contained and minimal expression of my dread and misery, then I would painstakingly apply make-up to the mask of coping that I wore each day. Off-stage I was dissolving. Looking back, I think that yes, I was mentally ill. But also that I was in a state of intense shock at the utter ransacking of my body and my life that even the happiest transition to motherhood brings. I would pace the floors in my dark house at night with a baby who felt like a stranger to me and I would genuinely wonder what we had done to our lives. And then I'd feel a deep sense of shame at so much as having this thought. It makes me angry that women are silenced on the reality of motherhood because all I needed (apart from psychiatric intervention) was someone to say,

'Don't worry we all have the "What the fuck have we done to our lives?" moment.' Instead we're imprisoned in this bizarre narrative of maternal bliss.

'Isn't it heaven?' asked a women I sat beside at a funeral when the baby was a few weeks old. *What the fuck is she talking about?* I remember wondering.

Now I know that for some women it is. Some women fall in love in the delivery room. Some babies arrive on a tidal wave of euphoria – I have had the luck to experience this now too and fuck, those birth hormones are potent. I have even gone on to think *Isn't this heaven?* myself on occasion when my babies invade the bed for morning cuddles which is, of course, an enormous relief after the bleak first year of motherhood. But in that moment at the funeral, while I grappled with my nipple and tolerated an older relative critiquing my latch, I wanted to run for it. To escape this so-called heaven.

The milk I produced began, to my mind, to feel tainted in some unidentifiable way. It was spoiled with my own madness and misery. How could it not be? This is why it's not working. I was never meant to be anyone's mother and this is why the baby hates me. I began to nurse, along with my squalling nervy baby, a powerful belief that I was infecting him with my sordid and sick self. The fact that breastfeeding is hard for a lot of people and it's not due to some nefarious sickness of their soul was not a fact that could penetrate my delusion at the time. The fact that

I couldn't perform this biological imperative was, to my compromised mind, like a compass pointing to true north. And my true north was that I was an aberration. Unfit. Ill. Mad. And sad.

The mechanics of breastfeeding feels like a dark art to me now: a confluence of faith, trust, biology and pure chance. Will the baby's mouth fit to your nipple? Will your let-down be a deluge? Or will your body be oddly withholding, as mine seemed to be? Why was it not working? Confirmation of the obscure and mysterious nature of breastfeeding seemed to come by how my breasts acted when the baby was not near. They were a new humming, buzzing force of their own, invigorated by their new function, however badly I thought they were performing it. At night between feeds, the breasts would rouse me just minutes before the shock of baby cries would pierce the silent house. How odd, I'd marvel. They know before I or even the baby knows that it is time. Later, when I was nursing my second baby, I was working in an office above a children's crèche and though I had weaned the baby of daytime feeds, the breasts would only have to hear childish shrieks and I'd feel the unmistakable ache of the let-down. *Oh* now *you're cooperating?*

Perhaps most telling of all was how in sync my breasts were with my own emotions. In the shower during my very contained and economical weeping each morning, milk would stream in sympathy from my breasts. How irredeemably, wonderfully weird – sometimes, the sight would nearly cheer me up. The salty tears would join the milky tears wending their way over my soft flaccid belly and on down to my legs where rust-coloured blood drained from my womb and pooled together at my feet. Salt, milk and blood.

The guilt of postnatal depression hasn't left me yet. Of every shame I harbour, none touches the shame of how I behaved in the first year of my first baby's life. He is seven now, an astonishing little person, and I still don't even dare to hope that he has escaped me. I worry that my spoiled milk will surely bubble up and boil over one day. How could it not?

The endless feasting at my useless tits left me wrung out both physically and mentally, but I couldn't give up. My obsession with making breastfeeding work had gone far beyond any immunity-boosting properties of breast milk and instead morphed into a symbol of every way I was failing as a mother.

And how could I not be failing, I now think, as I survey the very specific brand narrative of millennial mother-hood? Only occasionally are we starting to see the reality of motherhood portrayed in films and on TV. The portrayal of motherhood I saw even just seven years ago was vastly more sanitised. Why have we white-washed the less-palatable elements of motherhood? Because it is a woman's story. And men, for the most part, direct the stories. If we see a mother's struggle or weakness depicted in film, it is often within the context of the horror genre. This suggests to me that a mother being worn down by the demands placed on her or suffering from mental illness is still such a taboo subject that the only way we, as a society, have established to talk about such a common and normal experience is through the lens of horror – think *The Babadook*, *Carrie* or the *Ring* franchise and so many more. A mother is either a saint or deranged, with little in between.

We rarely find a nuanced depiction of the monstrous mother. And it's no coincidence the trope appears so frequently in books and film; the monstrous mothers are terrifying, of course they are. When a villain or ghostly entity is revealed to be a mother there is no more potent, unthinkable animal fear. We, the audience are forced to re-encounter the helplessness and confusion of childhood when our mothers were the universe. A mother gone wrong is the purest terror because her power over the child is infinite. Against such a woman, such a *thing*, there can be no defence.

The monstrous mother is a particularly terrifying thing for mothers themselves; it preys on our deepest fears of harming our children. And because the mothers are so often monstrous as a result of mental illness I see them as my kin and am therefore all the more terrified by them.

We rarely see a narrative offering redemption for a mentally ill mother recovering and continuing to raise her children. *Tully*, the 2018 film by Diablo Cody, attempted to shine a light on postnatal psychosis, which was helpful and I hope we will get more inclusion of these themes. However, *Tully* disappointed me a little. Rather than exploring postnatal psychosis directly in the film it was used as a device, a kind of 'big reveal' at the end. It is, of course, not an invalid way to explore the experience and we cannot hold up one film and demand it be all things to everyone. But I'd love for a celluloid mother to be sick and mad and to become well again and loving throughout. To be flawed and human.

Since I self-diagnosed as an utter failure of a mother, I have spoken to many women who were similarly ground down by this conviction that they were failing in early motherhood – it's a bit of an epidemic. Whether we hitched our perceived failure to the baby's immovable resistance to routine or sleep or feeding or the appearance of the dreaded colic, we all seemed to suffer to some extent from this chronic sense of our own poor performance.

In 2017, I was still searching tirelessly to be validated in my experience of motherhood as chaotic and tedious, terrifying and beautiful. I asked my friend, Jen, to do a podcast with me about it. She came up with the name *Mother of Pod*, a play on 'Mother of god!' an explosive phrase used, at least in Ireland, to communicate potent shock at whatever unbelievable event has just occurred. Can there possibly be a better description of the panicked incomprehension of new parenthood? Three years later, we are still recording. Apparently there is no end to the fresh hells of parenthood. (Jen and I also co-host *The Creep Dive* and crossover listeners have reported that *Mother of Pod* is scarier than anything on *The Creep Dive*. I definitely think it's gorier alright.)

In the years we've been recording we have heard from so many listeners deeply relieved that 'it's not just me'. No, it's not just you. It's not just me. We are all exhausted; we are all shaken; we are clueless. We're not monstrous. We all love them but fuck me, it's hard sometimes. And it is so much harder when nobody seems to be saying it. I actually think now there are thankfully so many more people being casually honest about parenthood, which is very comforting. Especially right now in this time when our parenting is so much more *visible* than previous generations.

We are the first people for whom our every day can be offered up as a performance on social media. Up until the 1950s the notion of 'childhood' as a concept was barely a thing, never mind a thing that needed to be cherished and preserved and made into an unforgettable magical experience as it is now. As a formless and pervading paranoia rises about the kinds of childhoods our children can even *hope* to have with the steady stream of violence, porn and injustice scrolling on our feeds, we are instating punishing timetables of betterment and *experiences* for our children, All to be recorded and published on the internet for the consumption of our peers, thus proving to friends and to total strangers that we're doing it 'right'. The sheer scope of comparison is exhausting. In previous generations, you might only have had your mother, your mother-in-law and Mrs O'Sullivan from across the road second-guessing your parenting efforts. Now there is an entire online community of 'perfect parents' to compete with, and yet more waiting to pounce on your every parenting misstep. It's exhausting.

This performance of motherhood on social media is a particularly fascinating element of the phenomenon, because of course women themselves are the authors on those platforms. I wonder, do the highly curated feeds with little reference to the emotional maelstrom that often accompanies the seismic shift to motherhood speak to our long tradition as women being the ultimate copers? Or do we simply long to be supported and validated in our choices in this unknown new landscape of pain and love and beauty and impossibly tiny socks?

People of the older generation can't hide their glee when we grapple with our children in their vicinity. We hug our children too much, or not enough. We're over-parenting by not letting them out of our sight, or neglecting them by being on our phones. Punishing schedules of early-morning crèche drop-offs are apparently to blame.

So often it seems that just taking your child into the public domain is basically akin to strolling around wearing a sandwich board proclaiming 'All Judgment Welcome! Feel Free to Get Vocal! Deride my Every Parenting Effort!'

If we aren't being directly accosted in the streets there's always online, where open letters to mums who may need a public scolding appear with irritating frequency. Think articles with headlines like 'Dear mum running into the shop and leaving your baby in the car' or 'Dear mum on her iPhone'. Not to mention the endless studies being released berating us for excessive screen time (ours and our children's), a dearth of outdoor play, working mothers, stay-at-home mothers, young mothers and women leaving our reproduction too late.

I think the problem is that women are demoted when they become mothers. If we stay at home to raise children, we are asked what do we do all day – as if looking after the children can be incidental to swanning around, having coffees and meeting friends. 'We are looking after children,' we want to scream. 'It is more work than your fucking board meeting.'

With this demotion, our position is usurped by our children. No longer are we the most important thing in our lives. We place our children above ourselves – as does society, which is why mothers are treated so pitilessly when they falter. In rejecting the demotion, the mother is breaking a primeval agreement. To be good and kind and perfect and loving and self-sacrificing, self-denying – or, even better! – self-*erasing*. And to deviate in any way is unacceptable, which is why to be anything other than perfect (impossible anyway) feels monstrous.

How more of us aren't driven mad by motherhood, I genuinely wonder.

SMOTHERHOOD

'"That was the night I decided to kill my mother."

'If I was ever to write a novel, that would be the opening line,' my mother announces quite out of the blue one day.

'Is it definitely a work of *fiction*?' I asked. Her mother hadn't died by this point, though it wasn't far off. I resolved then and there to steal the line from her as it is a very good one, but I've yet to employ it, opting instead for slightly less histrionic openers. I think I'm saving it for my foray into horror.

I was in the room with her when she got the call that her mother had died (of natural causes: I can categorically assure you my mother had no hand in it). I was surprised by my mother's reaction. She cried, which I've never seen her do very much. And she visibly sagged.

'I'm an orphan now,' she whimpered like a child as I put my arms around her.

We went together to see my grandmother in repose in the nursing home where she had died. It wasn't my first dead body, but it was the first I'd been so closely bonded to; this was about ten years before my dad died. I went in alone and startled at the sight in the bed – for a few disorientating moments I thought it was my own mother lying there. I had never thought they looked alike. My granny was large and solid and old all my life, while my mother is very small and slightly hyper and girlish in her demeanour. She is very pretty. I'm sorry to say I didn't find my granny pretty: I loved her and I thought she was impressive, but not pretty as such. But the face of her corpse was astoundingly youthful – all her wrinkles it seemed had been only kept in place by the tension of living and now they'd fallen away, allowing me quite suddenly to see the incredible resemblance between mother and daughter.

Momentarily seeing my mother in that deathbed gave me a fresh understanding of what it means to come from somebody. What that connection really does to us. I come from a body that once came from this body, and so on, like Russian Dolls for as far back as your mind can conceive. The men barely seem to come into it. Sure they come from these Motherships too, but then they scatter. They seem to be able to cut the cord in ways women don't. Is it because women understand their mothers in ways that men don't or can't? The mother–daughter line is something sturdier, more complex, more loving, more hateful than any other connection. I think of the umbilical cord, hitched to mother and child looking distinctly like something a Xenomorph might grow. What a crazy thing that women can produce to nourish their young. What an alien-like initial connection to have with our mothers. And then it's severed. (When I cut one of my own it was difficult; it took a few goes, like hacking through an extra-terrestrial pork loin.)

However, the connection remains, knitting mother and child together in an initial fierce co-dependence: the baby, after all, feasts on the mother continuously and equally the mother at times wants to devour the baby. This enmeshed state can resolve itself into a bond involving healthy distance or mutate into a dysfunctional dance of lifelong co-dependence. Or a little from column a) and a little from column b).

I would say I have caused my mother some of the greatest pain, irritation and worry of her life and she has inflicted similar on me. I would say it's practically unavoidable to be a daughter of any mother and not feel this to some degree, unless you have one of those cosy sorts of mothers who was always proffering lovely home-made scones without a generous side-helping of passive-aggression or impressively cutting remarks regarding face, clothes, life decisions or hair choices.

My mother has an almost mystical, telepathic personal connection with my hair. My hair could, if I were the malicious type, act as a voodoo doll for my mother. Any cut or tweak I might make to the hair wounds her as deeply as a thrust of a shiv in her side. 'Why do you insist on messing with your hair?' she cries, as though I've tattooed my face instead of gotten a trim and blow-dry.

How can I even begin to answer this question? Because I'm thirty-four years old? It was getting long? It's *my* hair?

How, I often wonder, does she even have the capacity to care this much about anything, never mind *hair*? I realise that's just the kind of boundless, obsessive love we have for our children. It's not rational. It reminds me of my own slightly raving love for my boys. It's a strange brand of superstitious mothering that I think I inherited from my mother, and she inherited from her mother before her. I picture it coursing down through the shimmering pork loin, a kind of pre-emptive catastrophising that we cling to in the hopes that will ward off unthinkable terrors and protect our children from calamity.

'If I worry enough about this one thing, then it definitely won't happen,' I try to explain to Seb, who doesn't understand. 'Say I'm worried that Rufus will grow up to be a psychopath, well if I worry about it enough then it definitely won't happen. It's never the things we're *thinking* about that blindside us and ruin our lives – it's always the one possibility that's never occurred to us, see?' He leaves me to it.

All my life, whenever my mother travelled she would send me letters explaining what to do when she inevitably died en route to wherever she was going.

I vividly remember receiving the first one aged sixteen. It began with the words: 'If you're reading this now then I didn't make it.' I glanced over to where she was, perfectly well and unscathed, making tea, and continued reading with interest. The rest of the letter was hilariously practical, listing various financial information and insurance details with little by way of grand declarations of love or life advice.

'I see you didn't make it.' I waved the letter at her; she snatched it up and tore it up. 'Aww but your bank account details ...'

I heard from my dad later that most of the trip had been blighted by anxiety about her imminent death and hijacked by bureaucratic details about how to time the posting of the letter so that it would not be stowed in the hold of their own doomed plane back to Ireland.

'She eventually posted from the airport right before we boarded the return flight,' he explained.

'Why didn't she just leave it on the dining room table?' I wondered.

'She didn't want you getting hold of any of the information.'

Ha. So essentially she loves me so much that she ruined a lovely holiday in Sicily fretting over my well-being after her untimely hypothetical death, but doesn't *trust* me enough with sensitive financial information.

'What does she think, that I'd kill her for the insurance money?'

My dad shrugged. 'If I was going to, I'd do it with trace amounts of arsenic – it builds up very slowly in the system. Very hard to detect,' he advised.

Over the years, she's switched to email and evidently become more trusting of both me and the ever-watchful Google. The subject line usually reads 'if I die' and the message is as practical and to the point as ever. But I can see her love in the sheer *labour* of all this worry and anxiety.

Marguerite Duras wrote that 'almost always, in all childhoods and in all lives that follow them, the mother represents madness. Our mothers always remain the strangest craziest people we have ever met.'

I'm sure in a book of stories confessing my own various strains of mental illness, she'll be very irritated that I've appointed *her* the mad one. And I do feel guilty about that: as the mother of a writer, she's been unfairly maligned in everything I've ever written. And being the wonderful mother that she is, she has largely put up with it, though when she read my last book, a novel, she did beg me to write a more sympathetic mother character next time.

'But my next work is a collection of non-fiction essays,' I told her.

She just nodded, sadly looking resigned and defeated. 'Of course it is,' she muttered ruefully and I felt a stab of guilt, albeit brief, as I flashed on the title of this very story.

I want to support my children in whatever they pursue but I'd probably prefer they become anything – Property developers! Clampers! Catholic priests! – rather than writers. It's just *dangerous* having a writer in the family.

It is, it has to be said, the ultimate self-sacrifice on her part to allow me to write about her at all. While evidently at one point she seemed to have very real concerns that I might murder her Menéndez brothers-style, I know that she loves me even more than my dad did. Perhaps 'more' is the wrong word but she certainly was more disposed to self-sacrifice than he ever was. We were once all on a long walk discussing whether or not we would give alibis on the other's behalf should we ever be in need of such a thing. My dad was willing but there was a 'but':

'I'm not offering up a blanket alibi – it'd have to be on a case-by-case basis. It would depend on the crime,' he concluded firmly.

My mother, on the other hand, looked me squarely in the eyes, training the full force of her special brand of fiercely loyal, slightly suffocating, smothering love on me and said:

'There's no caveats from me, I wouldn't prevaricate. You have an alibi from me any time you need it. No. Matter. What.'

Unnerving, but lovely all the same. And while I haven't put this promise to the ultimate test quite yet, she is always very sweet about lying to Seb for me. She's a very traditional feminist in that she believes women should have secret 'running away' money and lots and lots of time to themselves. If I involve her in any of my machinations (often involving secret trips to hotels to be by myself) she is always forthcoming with my alibis and is, I have to say, a frighteningly good liar.

When my father first became forgetful and eventualiy utterly dependent on her, she protected me fiercely from the full scale of the devastation at hand. She bore the first half of his decline alone while I roamed, lost and happy first in New Zealand, then in France. She never, ever asked me to come home. Quite the opposite, she encouraged the roaming, despite the solitude that surely had crept in around her in those years as her husband became childlike before her eyes. I was relieved I had her permission to stay gone. I didn't look forward to speaking to my dad on the phone; I resented his illness powerfully and any hint of it slipping into the long gaps as he searched for words or mangled facts like where I was living and who I was with would plunge me into a spoiled and selfish funk for days.

In those years when I was gone and he was going, my mother coped heroically. She'd have been more than entitled to partake in a little martyrdom – a right of all mothers I firmly believe – but she didn't. She stayed afloat, working and socialising with the same incredible stamina that she is known and admired for.

When I returned to Dublin in 2012, we resumed our hourly calls, texts and emails updating one another on scraps of newly acquired gossip, who was being an asshole to us on any given day and what nice dress we'd just seen and wanted to buy. In short, we reverted to our smothering brand of co-dependency and remained largely entwined for the next few years, hammering at the coalface of my father's illness, comrades in the exhausting work of grief and denial.

At the end of 2013, when my first son was born, she called me every morning to see how the night before had gone. She gamely took my side against the baby whenever I said he was being a prick that day or some variation of such.

'You're absolutely right, they are the worst,' she said loyally of the baby she was and still is obsessed with.

We passed hours visiting my father together. I would tell her when I was visiting (never enough) so that she could take a break, but she would still always go too. We visited him in the psychiatric ward, the dementia ward, the nursing home and then the room in the nursing home where they keep the industrial air-freshener and the reclining chairs and you know you are on the homestretch of the suffering by then.

In 2017, we came together at my father's deathbed for a thirty-hour marathon goodbye. By this point we'd spent what felt like a lifetime watching his decline, while bemoaning the terrible coffee available in the nursing home. At some point, we'd become virtually impervious to the suffering we were witnessing and indifferent to each other's grief. You have to.

Practically every time we sat with my dad together, at some point she would turn to me mid-conversation apropos of nothing and say: 'If I ever get like this,' we'd both look at my dad, vacant in his chair or bed, 'promise me, you'll smother me with a pillow.'

The first time she made this request, I think I laughed and said it would be my pleasure. By the hundredth time she said it I was a person who'd given long consideration to euthanasia, and while I agreed with it in theory I couldn't risk jail-time with two small children to care for.

'Promise me you'll smother me, if I ever get like this.'

'No! If we're not smothering him,' I'd indicate my dad suspended in his vegetative state, 'and he *really* deserves it, why should you get the easy exit? And I'd be the one risking everything by pillowing you. Absolutely not.'

But something tells me she'd probably manage to guilt me into it. Maybe she's storing up that martyrdom she didn't deploy when I was travelling and left her alone with my dad's illness. She's banked it for when she's trapped in an adult nappy and wants out.

And maybe I can picture it. Smothering her, I mean. In the most loving way imaginable, of course. The way she has smothered me.

'That was the night I decided to kill my mother …'

Of course, my alibi dies with her.

PART 5
FINAL GIRL

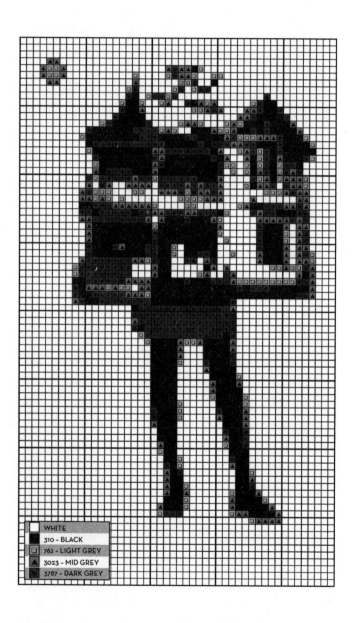

WHITE
310 – BLACK
762 – LIGHT GREY
3023 – MID GREY
3787 – DARK GREY

NEEDLE GIRLS

To begin, I need to give you a picture of where I am. I need to give you this because work spaces, studios, offices feel relevant. I am in my office. I am inordinately proud of my office. It's a space I felt I had to graduate to. Before I had this place, I worked in libraries and in my bedroom in the attic. In corners, in the car and on my phone in the dark while my milk drip-dripped into a baby mouth. Now I have a desk in a room, where there is space to make my work, work that really isn't work at all but more a compulsion. I have at last been able to arrange all my books in proper shelves. And even the books that I have written are displayed here on a modest, out-of-the-way shelf. And those books are full of the words that I drip-dripped onto their pages. In front of me are the books I am reading for this book. And my jotter and pen for the lines that spill into my head endlessly and that don't have a place yet. Obviously my laptop and coffee are here. And the lavender that I always pick for luck – a little superstitious incantation to send me the will to write, because that wanes too.

To my right is what I call my Murder Wall. You know the wall in movies, on which the demented inner workings of the killer's mind is mapped out? These are the plans for the books that at a certain point need to be ripped free from the jotter and displayed side by side. I need to see the full picture of what must then be knit slowly word by word. It's a pattern. Fittingly, below the murder wall is the current knitting project. It's a sleeve. Or what will be a sleeve – a disembodied arm taking shape and growing from the needles.

Making is such a basic human impulse that I think we've become a bit estranged from. When people talk about the epidemic of mental illness there is often an inference that new generations are not as hardy as older ones, or that the epidemic we are really living in is one of over-diagnosis. But to me, it makes perfect sense that our minds are struggling more and more as we move further away from the natural world and into a simulated one online. While our imprint on the world now lasts forever on the internet, there is far less tangible, real-world evidence of our existence. Think of the relics we have from our mothers and grandmothers. In a patchwork quilt or needlepoint piece, the author of such a creation has handled and touched every square inch. They willed it into being, either with intense concentration or easy, absent-minded love.

When I was in a mental hospital, I attended occupational therapy and thought, *Huh, are we so divorced from the everyday act of creating and making that it must be prescribed to us?* In occupational therapy, we collected things like leaves and flowers to draw, we could tend to a garden or bake. One of the most interesting things we did was a class in doodling: the therapist would draw a large doodle and we copied every line with fine pens onto very tiny tiles of cardboard. This kind of therapy is essentially, as its title suggests, occupation. Occupation is something that can fall out of reach when you're sick in the head. And we can easily forget that the most basic things are what's missing whether it's a shower or brushing your teeth. Or if it is simply finding comfort and order in doodling or, in my case, knitting. Knitting seems to slow the racing in my head. The order and precision that's required helps me find ease.

Knitting and writing are now twinned for me. So much of writing is not writing at all, but rather resolving. Resolving the characters, resolving the plot, resolving the shapeless thing you're sure is something but hasn't come into focus yet. During these seemingly empty stretches of my occupation, I knit. I order the stitches to order the words. Knitting and writing have the same kind of rhythm. Sometimes stitches and words flow almost automatically and sometimes there's a snarl or a knot to dwell or a pattern to pore over.

When I write, I wear a cardigan-blanket hybrid that was an early knitting project of mine. It isn't lovely exactly, but it is warm and cosy. On my feet are the first, endearingly misshapen socks I ever made. After a year or so of knitting, I had to start punishing unsuspecting friends and family with my wares. Our house just couldn't accommodate my output. And Seb was complaining that we were living in a plague of fluff. Which definitely affected him more than me, given the fluff seemed especially drawn to him and was constantly attached, velcro-like, to his beard. I don't feel any attachment to the things I make after they're done, and I'll happily inflict them on others. I do feel like I'm passing on slightly cursed objects given everything I make is imbued with my neuroses. I've made haunted blankets for babies and haunted hats for my friends and haunted jumpers for my family.

Some people knit for the end result and some, like me, simply for the occupation. Serial killers often fall into one of two categories: either they are process killers or product killers. I think knitters are like this too: you either are in it for the sensation of doing or you are in it for the finished piece.

Process killers are your sadistic killers – think Richard Ramirez or the Toy Box Killer. For them, the act of taking a life itself is what they crave. Meanwhile, product killers don't necessarily enjoy the killing but are in it for the end result. Take Jeffrey Dahmer and his dead 'lovers' that would 'never leave'. Or Ed Gein who wanted women's skin to make garments, household items and inventive reupholstery projects.

If you are unnerved by the turn this has taken, don't be (and of course you're not after the bloodbath of previous pages). I started knitting around the same time we started *The Creep Dive*. The show was initially about us investigating and reporting on the lesser-known creeps of the internet, but it quickly evolved into us coming out as Creeps ourselves. And it's proved cathartic. Revealing our ghoulish passions as a way to purge them, to normalise them. Naming the frightening thing goes some way towards neutering its awful power.

I've always been obsessed with these things. In primary school, I spent break times telling horrifying stories about dismemberment and cannibalism. Not ghost stories as such because little me felt ghosts, while definitely not a welcome addition to any home, were not that scary because they couldn't hurt us. But people? People were the nightmare.

In my teens, tales of true-life horror were not a simple Google search away, so I mostly kept my creep flag under wraps because the stuff I wanted to explore seemed more like the preserve of future spree killers than the kind of topics young women picked over. What I've since learned is that there were a whole lot of us creeping through the newspapers and trashy magazines trying to glean the disturbing details of any crime that might take place; we were just doing it quietly so as not to perturb anybody.

Why women obsess over true crime is a question that's been posed many times in the years since the genre hit the mainstream and exploded. I think there are two answers. One, these grim stories are the few in which women are almost guaranteed to be the protagonist. Disturbing and depressing as this fact is, these stories are more likely than any fiction or film to pass the Bechdel Test. If women want to read about women, it's a good genre. Secondly, I think because women are so often the targets of these crimes, we have an unconscious drive to gather intel on how to survive these horrors. The message often implied is that these deaths could have been avoidable if only the women hadn't gone down a dark alley, lived alone, worn a dress, driven somewhere in a car or been near a man. And so we still find ourselves amassing our knowledge, listening to true crime podcasts and watching documentaries to research our own survival.

When I was younger, due to the lack of Murderpedia, I instead obsessed over horror movies and books. My mother despaired of this unfeminine addiction, just like she despaired of my adoration of Jackie Chan movies when I was a karate-loving five-year-old. However, as much as she likes to pretend otherwise, I'm certain my morbidity is connected to my mother: she of the no-caveats, no-strings alibi. My mother wouldn't see herself as a lover of the creepy and bizarre, but most every conversation we have is kicked off with some horrendously tragic anecdote. This is quite possibly a facet of the Irish Mother in general. My mother likes to offload them on me, in exactly the same way that before *The Creep Dive*, I routinely offloaded them on my husband.

A typical phone call with my mother:

> My mother (lamenting tone): I suppose you saw what happened in Cork.
>
> Me: No, no I didn't. And honestly if it's bad I don't want—
>
> My mother: Those poor children, can you believe—
>
> Me: Please no!
>
> My mother: You just wouldn't think a little thing like a curtain pull cord could lead to—
>
> Me: Please, I said I don't want to know!
>
> My mother: Can you imagine the parents right now?
>
> Me: I feel sick. Thank you for filling me with this sadness and horror.
>
> My mother: What are ye having for dinner?

After I hang up, I immediately locate Seb.

Me: Did you hear what happened in Cork?

Seb: NO. I'm not listening. Do not say another word.

So you see, finding a repository for all the horror that I gather and contain has been as much for my marriage as it has been for my mental health. Why the attraction to such frightening things? It might seem odd given my head all by itself can be such a horror show. But it has come to make a skewed kind of sense to me.

In the rooms of my head, some are like Bluebeard's room, cacophonous with depravity, ghastly but obvious somehow. Other rooms are filled with familiar things that are warped somehow. Uncanny and unnerving. Other spaces are the darkness beneath the cellar door, more frightening than the known can ever be. Hauling out the horror, putting a name or story to the formless anxiety, gives it a boundary, a tangible parameter, and ultimately disarms it.

In the book *IT* by Stephen King, it is the shape-shifting, unquantifiable nature of the horror that makes it so haunting and terrifying. I feel the same about my mental illness. It roams my head, sometimes taking the shape of intrusive thoughts that echo in the halls, sometimes a powerful idea I cannot shake that seems at odds with reality and sometimes a life-threatening, fatal emptiness.

The scariest stories are the ones where the monster is hidden, its deeds unclear and the fate of its victims unknown. This is what has made the faceless Slenderman so compelling. In all the fiction and art Slenderman has inspired, few versions offer any definition of the kind of wicked entity he is. The stories are restrained when it comes to gore, the endings obscure and all the more frightening for it.

Gathering, cataloguing and sharing the horrors of the outside world is something tangible to do in the face of all this unknown. It is as meditative and therapeutic as guiding yarn through needles and fingers to make first one stitch then another and another until the excess of what – nerves? energy? mania? hyperactivity? – dissipates. I find the additional buzz of my head can be turned down to a manageable volume with just this simple action. Whatever the buzz is, so much of the time it is benign, even helpful. Like a flame lit in a dark room, it can reveal to me the words and ideas that I love. However, on occasion that same amazing flame can catch fire and erupt into an inferno. Like the mood stabilisers and antidepressants, the knitting and the creeping brings me into harmony. It takes me from boiling down to a simmer and makes me more manageable. To myself, that is. I knit so that I don't unravel. I think a lot of people would say this too.

We had been doing *The Creep Dive* for about a year when the pandemic hit. Before that we were doing live shows of our gleeful horror schtick and meeting like-minded Creeps wherever we went. It was astonishing to us that not only did people listen to our podcast, they came to see us and wanted to meet us. It was amazing. We didn't really realise it then, but a community was gathering. During lockdown, we all got together every Thursday night to do the show live over Zoom and got to know the people who regularly came. We were all Creeps, yet the environment was very welcoming and friendly – it makes me wonder if those cannibal forums on the Dark Web are actually lovely inclusive spaces after all. Though of course they're inclusive – they're cannibals, they can't be picky. I think our weekly virtual meet-up was a bit like communal therapy; it was for me anyway. A brief escape from the anxiety and bleakness that had settled outside our homes and inside our heads.

Listening to a podcast is not your average internet para-social relationship. There is a connection there that comes much closer to friendship. We began to know the Creeps and they us. When we talked about our favourite sweets on the show, the treats came flooding in by post. Our Creeps are inordinately talented, and many have drawn incredible pictures of us or the characters we talk about. A lexicon of complex references and jokes has evolved. There's a book-club and a WhatsApp group, both entirely independent of us. The Creeps have sent us Christmas presents and baby gifts. During the course of *The Creep Dive*, Cassie has started a business and moved house, Jen has moved house and had a baby, and I have had a baby and two breakdowns. The first of these probably went unnoticed, but during the second I went into hospital and missed two weeks of recording. When I returned, I was by no means better yet, but creeping was the first thing I wanted to do when I got out of the hospital. To be with my friends and the Creeps and do what we always do: marvel at the horror, haul it out, mould it into a contained story with a beginning, middle and end. And, of course, laugh at it where we can.

We eventually noticed that a huge amount of the Creeps craft. So much so that during the first lockdown of the Covid-19 pandemic, we instated *The Craft Dive* on Sunday nights, a Zoom where sometimes as many as seventy people would show up to knit or paint or crochet or make jewellery – one Creep even wrote code for the duration. We would show off our projects and tell awful, just awful, stories.

And telling the awful stories makes them more manageable, distilling them and resulting in something tangible. I think knitting shares this. Knitting gives time a tactile form. It takes something, perhaps dark and furious, from your mind, arranges it and forms it into a harmless object. It's the same with embroidery and so many other crafts. Giving my hands something to do is an obvious way to temporarily cure me of myself. As they push needles through wool and aida, they can't do any harm. They are safely confined. They can't pick up a drink or drag fists and nails across skin. Lately my self-harm is being reformed and I'm bringing my needles to my body to make enduring marks to be proud of. When I see what I make, the cross stitch, the wonky hats, the embarrassing pictures, I see that I am giving expression to the nebulous, the infirmity that is mental illness.

I remember feeling the potency of Stephen King's *IT* dwindle when it assumed a corporeal form. A big spider is frightening, but there's a route through the horror. Kill it with fire. When IT is called Pennywise, get it with a silver bullet. When IT has a name, it has a boundary. It is not infinite horror, it is surmountable.

I never had a name for what was wrong with my head. Frequently the poles seemed to shift, a sort of mental subsidence. I tended to keel every few months or years; my own horizon wasn't something I could depend on. Unnamed it petrified me. Would I always have it? Would it be the end of me ultimately? Would I infect my children with it? And what, oh what, even was it?

I got a name for it this year. At thirty-five, I got a name and a new set of meds and a slight reframing of what has been nearly fifteen years of the unknown. It hasn't fixed it but I've got a better sense of the terrain of this thing. It is nameable now and somewhat quantifiable.

BAD TIMING II

The apocalypse, when it comes, looks nothing how any of us thought it would. The zombie onslaught is not quite as cinematic; the peril is largely invisible. We are deeply frightened, as much by the virus itself as the uncertainty. Survival of the human race rests, it seems, not on overt heroism but the fairly ho-hum hand-washing.

'I thought the end would be more exciting than this,' I whine to my husband. Ireland's first lockdown is announced two weeks after the birth of our third child. The isolation will not eradicate the virus, but is essential to stem the flow of stricken bodies to hospitals.

I am in my car when news of schools and crèches closing comes through. I'm parked at the beach, laptop in lap, finishing edits on my second novel. The third baby is asleep in the backseat. The announcer on the radio sounds as bemused reading out the information as I feel hearing it. There's even perhaps a shiver of nervous excitement, though I can't imagine how I will work with three small children at home. Driving to get the baby to sleep and tapping away in my car had been my game plan to get this book finished. Some would say less than ideal circumstances to begin with.

Of course, the timing is terrible. Even now, months later, after the restrictions of the first lockdown have eased and I have (I think/hope) cleared my fourth significant breakdown, I can't help but feel that timing and circumstances conspired against me. A third baby and a book to finish would be manageable. Throw in the pandemic and I'm out.

Timing is not this baby's strong suit, arriving as he did three weeks early and three times faster than the last baby had. The birth was breathtaking. Wild and fast, I was just a limp participant succumbing to a quake, marooned on the bed. Two young midwives hurried back and forth battening down for an approaching disaster. *Blankets, adjust the trace, check, check, check.* The final three contractions hurled me open as I vomited into a paper hat and felt the baby's body shift down inside my own. It was euphoric and barbaric in equal measure. Like it always is. My husband looked shocked as I pitched and thrust in the bed and opened my mouth to roar like an animal at the ceiling. A moment to laugh at his stunned face before the next one came rolling in and on the crest of this cracking force, my body unleashed the baby. Fucking A.

Two hours and no tear! I was elated. A new boy to wonder at. I was jangly at the unexpected turn this Monday morning had taken. A look back to this date in my inbox shows me replying to a work email with no mention of the rush hour of my own.

They took the baby from me shortly after.

It was emotional whiplash. Like running full tilt only to screech to a stop at the edge of a sickening drop. One minute he was wrapped neatly in the bed beside me, the next a nurse was returning empty-handed and talking about the high-dependency unit. His absence was an anathema to me. I immediately began the kind of superstitious bargaining that makes perfect sense to all catastrophists, and little to anyone else.

This was all my fault. I hadn't worried enough to safeguard my little baby. My husband couldn't fathom my conviction that I had caused this. He doesn't agree that outcomes can be affected by my banking angst to safeguard us from impending doom. The physical sensation of being separated from our babies is destabilising. To anyone around me, the baby was experiencing something reasonably commonplace and routine while, to me, the previously safe and impossibly lucky life I'd lead was in jeopardy. I was experiencing a dreadful new normal, an alternate, perilous reality where the worst had happened.

In my body, the panic was total. I was perched at the agonising moment of falling; the adrenaline was flooding through me. I was convinced that my tiny baby was dying. I stayed frozen in this moment for the three days he lay still and perfect in the NICU. At every turn, I was reassured that this was a routine blip, but I couldn't trust them. I was certain that if I abandoned my vigil of worry and began to believe in him, that would be the exact moment he would be snatched from me. This all made perfect sense to me. I was scared to hold the baby – it seemed too risky to interfere in the little plastic case where he lay gradually unfurling, tendril-like wires creeping away from him. When we were told he was going home, I finally exhaled. A stay of execution. A bullet dodged.

The terror swoops into elation. He is mine. He will be okay. I bring him home to the bed under the eaves where we stay for several days.

A new baby makes me do funny things. Write poetry and the like.

These next words were written from a small, exquisite moment in my life one month before my thirty-fifth birthday and two weeks before the pandemic would derail everything for everyone:

It is early on a February evening. Rain hits the slanted window in my attic bedroom. To my left lies a huge swathe of soft downy wool – a blanket still hitched to knitting needles. To my right, a velvet baby boy sighs occasionally. He was knit from my womb. Though he is no longer hitched to me, our bodies are a duet still. Notes of milk slip into his sweet mouth, the pulse of his fontanelle and flickering eyelids form a tiny percussion.

On the floor below, the rowdy boys are bounding. They seem colossal since the new boy's arrival. Guttural monster noises drift up the stairs. Then a loving threat: 'I'm going to pinch that little bottom,' Seb warns amid delighted cries.

The loom inside hangs empty. I feel rearranged and cavernous, though an imperceptible shift means this negation will soon be enclosed once more. For now, though, I am agape. Wide open. I feel boundary-less and border-less – like an element. It is an exposing and vulnerable state.

Two weeks later the lockdown was called. Bad timing.

As the virus gains ground, the lockdown feels less and less temporary. When I make my weekly trek to the supermarket, I deliberately go in search of disaster movie moments, to confirm that this strange new life is indeed happening out in the real world and not just on an ever-more nihilistic Twitter feed. The edge of the city centre is within my government-sanctioned radius and I cycle down the centre of deserted streets feeling the shiver of the uncanny. A huge digital display that usually advises on traffic delays now simply displays beseeching messages to 'Wash your hands' and 'Stay at home'.

The pandemic protocol on the face of it seems like it should be easy. Stay at home. Limit contact. Wear a mask. Designate the person who shops for the household. Practise social distancing. Yet rapidly the lockdown reveals our childlike dependence on normality, on both routine and variety to give life that essential flavour – the umami that keeps us hungry and happy, engaged and alive.

Animals in captivity often display repetitive, functionless behaviours. Watching my six-year-old pace the yard, I feel a palpable grief for what he is going through. It reminds me of a haggard tiger I once saw in a zoo – not a place I think I'll ever feel right visiting again. The tiger also paced; it had a funny head-shaking movement and bald patches that further reading makes me think might have been as a result of over-grooming – another example of repetitive, functionless behaviour that is often seen in captive animals. 'Captivity' seems like a slightly hysterical word to use for what we experience in lockdown, but downplaying the trauma and denying the impact of that strange stagnant season feels like a disservice.

I think a lot of how we will reflect on this time when we've put some distance between then and wherever now is. There will be aftershocks surely. A vaccine is on the horizon, but we cannot vaccinate against the trauma.

With a crisis of such magnitude, there is no end to the different genres of suffering. My husband and I express our gratitude that our dads had died before the pandemic. That they, and we, were spared loving someone vulnerable and delicate through that dangerous era. We didn't have to attend a dystopian funeral where the celebration of life was utterly stymied by restrictions. That we didn't have to leave them in a care home, praying the virus wouldn't breach the walls. Still, as much as I took near daily inventory of how much worse my situation could be, I was a wreck and constantly berating myself for not coping when others had it so much worse.

At any given moment, from my pit of self-pity I implored myself: think of the essential workers; think of the frontline healthcare providers; think of the old; think of the young, the poor, the employed, the unemployed, the business-owners, the homeless, the people with underlying conditions. The various inventive ways the pandemic annihilated us would have been impressive if it were not so devastating.

Depression is a blank tide. It erases: hope, possibility, potential, nothing survives when the dark waters advance. In this way we were experiencing a unique event, a depression of global proportions. Beyond the physical toll of Covid-19, the true devastation was a pandemic of despair.

Everywhere people were experiencing profound loss. The loss of loved ones, of sharing their new baby with their family, of celebrating a marriage, of stability. And just because it wasn't the worst it could possibly be didn't mean it wasn't hard and didn't hurt. We were grieving everything from our old pre-pandemic hair to the lives we expected to be living and everything in between. There is no feelings quota. Being sad about our shitty situation was not depriving someone else of being sad about their life.

Occasionally at the height of lockdown, I would encounter someone having a relatively 'good pandemic'. Intolerable. These people would make the mistake of saying they were loving the 'break' from routine and were getting loads of reading and TV done. This would immediately see me playing pandemic bingo. Tallying up who was worse off – a kind of Tetris of hardship. One of my friends had only one child to manage, but she lives in an apartment, so had no garden. I, meanwhile, had three kids to care for but no dishwasher. Often I would recognise that the true irony of the pandemic was how one person's fantasy was another's hell. My friends who were isolating alone were, from my perspective, experiencing the actual dream, while for their part they probably just wanted some fucking company.

Still when I looked at my little section of society, my pacing boys and my tiny baby, my exhausted husband and my own wrecked face, I felt that families were screwed in the apocalypse.

We made up a significant cog in the national 'keep the show on the road' machine. We made up a large part of the workforce; we were the entire education and childcare solution. It was exhausting. So much so that even now, months later, I am still bone tired. Weary on a cellular level.

At one point, a woman I know on Instagram asked me if I would record a video of my daily life as a working mother in lockdown for a project she was doing. I was tempted to just send her the opening scenes of *Apocalypse Now*. What was family life like in pandemic? The word that keeps coming up is 'relentless'.

My husband and I drop-kicked children and laptops and home-school assignments and scooters and bikes and Lego and phones back and forth at each other all day long. We were constantly one foot in an inbox or Zoom meeting. The only real break was the two hours of respite provided by the film we put on for our kids every day at 4pm. Though calling that 'respite' is a joke, as we desperately tried to get on top of our separate jobs and still care for our newborn. Bedtime for the kids meant finally we only had one child to mind, though for me – the food source for said child – 7pm–10pm was a marathon of fussing, pacing, swaying, rocking, breastfeeding, winding, crying and attempting to watch TV. At 10pm, nothing particularly changed but I relocated to bed to commence the night portion of the 24-hour, seven-days-a-week shitshow. So yeah: *Apocalypse Now,* but with more screaming.

Two-and-a-half months into the pandemic I googled: 'Is it postnatal depression or pandemic?' The baby was three months old at this point. Unsurprisingly, the results were not particularly satisfying. It seemed, according to one article, that the pandemic was providing 'perfect conditions' for postnatal depression. Wonderful.

In the months of lockdown, I never considered that I too have an underlying condition. On and off over fifteen years I've been treated for my mental illness. It's always been a knotty thing to name, starting as it did with that bad drug trip in 2007; it has taken many forms from the hallucinatory to the paranoid to the depressed. Fun times. An upside of being so mental for so long is that in lockdown I was very connected with support. My psychiatrist took my calls – we debated changing my medication but agreed that messing with that critical alchemy in lockdown could be too volatile. I also attended regular group therapy over Zoom. Still I worried. I worried about the advance of my dark waters, my own claustrophobic ocean of fear and disquiet.

Drowning often doesn't look like drowning. In the minutes before someone drowns, a paradoxical instinctive response kicks in that means the person can no longer wave their arms or shout for help. This means even those relatively nearby may not actually realise the person is just about to succumb. Sometimes coping can be similarly deceptive.

The 'feelings apocalypse' is how I jokingly come to describe the Covid world. I go about my days assuming everyone is similarly bowed beneath the weight of their feelings. And then one sunny Friday morning, I am hospitalised with it.

Ironically the second I am shut away, the roar in my head also seems to shut off and recede. I'm left with an oddly blank landscape, the kind that immediately precedes a tsunami. As I pick my way across the featureless shore, queuing for breakfast, for meds, for vitals check, I wonder with distant curiosity when the tsunami will hit. For the most part I am not scared – I am too numb for that. Finally at dawn on day six, as I cradle the mechanical baby that has accompanied me to hospital, a breast pump to drain my milk five times a day, I break. I am so frightened. The fright is drowning me. A kind of choking, inner waterboarding. I am shocked to my fingertips by how potent this fear is. A ripple of cold, harsh terror slips through my veins, spiders out through my body every time I think of where I am, what has happened, how beyond the walls of the hospital three small babies need me to be well.

Fucking fuck.

The timing of this breakdown was better than most, I have to say. My husband and I had been about to down tools to spend a week down the country with my mother and our kids. The fact that I can look very well, wildly fantastic even, the second before breaking down means they were as surprised as I was at the detour I was taking into psychiatric care.

303

I didn't know what to pack. I was quiet during the admission process. Then skittish in my room as a nurse went through my belongings to remove chargers and my knitting needles. I itched at the knitting being taken. *I need them, they make my head bearable*, I wanted to plead, not thinking of their other uses, not thinking of why I was even in there. Not even pondering how unbearable things had felt for some time.

'You'll probably get them back, when you're ready.' She was kind. I just smiled and then explained the mass of wires and tubes that constitute a double breast pump laid out on the bed between us.

'If I stop feeding all of a sudden my boobs will freak out,' I explained. This too was taken for a short time until I was deemed less of a risk.

Throughout admission, a conviction persists in my head. *You are being ridiculous.* The tone is scathing. *You are taking up a bed that someone actually needs, Sophie. You have definitely been more suicidal than this before.*

In the hospital, I immediately set about staging a committed (*ba-doom*) performance of my most ludicrous 'I'm fine' show yet. Performing for an audience of who? I'm not even sure.

'How are you feeling?' The nurse in the dining room asks at lunch.

'I'm fine, great!' I chirrup stupidly. I'm clutching a plastic tray, queuing for lunch in a psychiatric ward, but obviously I'm completely fine. Context matters and in the confines of the mental hospital, even mundane things can take on the appearance of madness. My thumb-sucking, for example, is doing me no favours. There is a pitch-and-putt course out the back of the hospital and my new friends on the ward are locked into a toxic obsession with incrementally improved scores. Madness. I resist their invitations to golf and instead spend most mornings running loops on the leafy path around the pitch-and-putt course.

I like running but as is so often my way I can turn even the most benign things into a toxic crutch. Most days I am running between 10 and 15km. I run from breakfast to lunch. I even round down the number of loops I have done if anyone asks so as not to attract too much attention. After running, I eat lunch and anxiously locate the next thing I can do. I sense I am slightly missing the point when one of my roommates remarks on how much I do in a day. I don't have my laptop, though I do write my newspaper column on my phone. I am drawing, painting, knitting and doing yoga – I sheepishly admit that 'It might be kind of why I'm in here.'

The doing subdues me. The running pounds out some of the unmanageable momentum of my head. On the fourth day, a boy on the ward asks me why I'm on a particular drug. 'It slows my thoughts down, makes my head more manageable.'

'No,' he is unequivocal in his response. 'You don't say that. That sounds mad. You must say, "It helps me with my daydreams."'

This boy is a favourite of mine here: no reproduction of our encounters would ever capture his spirit, his undeniable comedic flair or frequent cutting and hilarious drags. He petitions his doctors for release with emails written in verse and escapes frequently. He is assigned a one-to-one nurse who hovers nearby at all times and presumably gets the full benefit of this boy's patter.

'Saying it helps me with my daydreams sounds way madder,' I goad him, simply to prolong our chat.

A nurse passes and explains a new doctor will see the boy today. 'You'll like him, he's very well spoken,' she says.

'Good. So am I,' the boys snaps, not missing a beat.

He is right. The *daydreams* are helped by the drugs, but with the bad, the good are gone too, and I feel shut off from myself. When my wry and composed psychiatrist appears on the ward a few days after my arrival, he seems amused. He is just back from holidays.

'Sophie! What happened?' He says this in the way you might say, *I leave you for one bloody week!*

'I honestly don't know what happened. I thought I was going along great. I was busy, getting loads done, totally on top of everything. Then it all just seemed to veer off a cliff.' Just explaining this I am aware of trying to sound normal, though my words are slippy, spilling out over one another.

'When it's going well it feels amazing in my head. It feels like riding a horse. Have you ever ridden a horse and gone from a canter up into a gallop and it feels incredible? It feels like you're flying. And then I dunno, it's like the reins are out of my hands and then I just crash.'

My psychiatrist is reassuring.

'It's probably good timing that you're here right now, Sophie. Because we can perhaps better understand how your head works. You're a well-put-together person. You operate at a high frequency. And that's a good thing. That helps you in your work.'

I'm nodding, trying not to blurt out anything weird. In a perfectly ordinary social occasion, I can say all the left-field things I want without fear that it'll be noted on some file somewhere.

'You've a great colour,' I say, unable to help myself. Luckily he's used to me.

'What happens after the galloping?'

'I just feel so nothing, so numb. There's just this hanging darkness blighting my days. And I get so low. Like, if there's a state of, like, ambient suicidal, that's how I get. Like if there was a way that it wouldn't, ya know, destroy everyone I love. I suppose I'm saying if there was a switch I could flick that would just turn off life, that'd be great. So I guess, suicidal, but in a lazy way.'

In the end, I spend just two weeks there. And spend the rest of the summer nostalgic for the ward. Isn't that funny? Isn't it even funnier that the word 'nostalgic' means pain of an old wound?

I didn't want to go there. While I was there I obsessed about getting out and now all I think about most days is how much I want to be back there. The ward was so simple. Everything was out of my hands and what a relief that was. I was contained. I couldn't do any damage.

Out here in the world, there are people I am essential to. This is terrible to a person like me. It's a fact I use against myself frequently. *You don't deserve these beautiful boys*, I bully myself. *You don't deserve their love.* These thoughts are my illness.

Once a woman wrote to me to ask if I felt it was irresponsible to have children if you are mentally ill. It is a question that takes more than even a book to answer. It takes a life. And I will spend my own life debating it, but perhaps awareness of that will go some way towards making it okay that I am someone's mother. When you are a mother, your body is a home. Right now, just months after the breakdown, I am a dilapidated one. In one room hangs the empty loom, in another, the scraps of work I have pushed and pushed to create in this cursed year. My sons clatter through looking for me. My husband looks for me too. He searches my shuttered eyes.

My oldest boy kisses me on the mouth so hard it hurts. I yelp in pain and surprise. And I wonder: is this his way of drawing me back?

I am coming.